My
American Transformation
Reminiscences from a Time of Wonder

S. Mena

"I believe in America. America has made my fortune: a free life to pursue my every dream and achieve those things for which I was willing to work, to worship freely, to express myself without trepidation or fear of reprisal, to travel freely within and without its borders and to amass a collection of experiences that have made me the person I've become."

- Jorge Mena

My American Transformation
Reminiscences From a Time of Wonder

Copyright © 2019 by S. Mena

ISBN: 978-1-696-73761-6
Printed in USA by AMG Publishing

Dedication

To Michael, Alex, Eric, Nicolas, Patrick and Nathan. The next chapter is yours to write.

Table of Contents

Preface

In the opening scene of Francis Ford Coppola's movie, *The Godfather*, Bonasera, sits in front of the Don's desk and says, "I believe in America. America has made my fortune. And I raised my daughter in the American fashion." So did my father, except he raised two sons.

I too believe in America. America has made my fortune: a free life to pursue my every dream and achieve those things for which I was willing to work, to worship freely, to express myself without trepidation or fear of reprisal, to travel freely within and without its borders and to amass a collection of experiences that have made me the person I've become.

I raised six sons in the *"American fashion"* of which Bonasera speaks. Fostering a love for this land chosen above all others. Instilling in them a knowledge that anything is possible in our beloved America and that God, family and country are the three most important words in a man's life. It is for them and for the generations to follow that I thought it wise to commit to paper some of my recollections of this evolution that led me to become an American—remembrances that now grow dim as the years add scores of new entries into the annals of my life.

While initially there are political observations in the first essays, they are not meant to expound philosophical views, only a retelling of my experiences in a communist country that lead us to seek a better life in our adoptive home. And while my intent is to share the purest recollections of my mind, I doubt that with the passage of time and that with the repeated telling of each incident that there has not been an enhancement of the details relating to the events recorded herein. Nonetheless, these are my memories of key formative moments in my life.

CHAPTER 1

Apodaca Street

It is as indelible an imprint as an eleven-year-old mind is capable of enduring. The car was a late fifties Buick well preserved by its owner, my mother's paternal grand-uncle, *"Tío Doro."* He slowly drove us over the unpaved road of Apodaca Street. It was a solemn moment. Even one as young as I, knew that this was an important event, one that would forever change our lives.

For some reason, the smell of the brown, heavy wool suit that my mother had sewn for me is still the first thing that comes to mind of that day decades later. The unusually heavy fabric for our Caribbean island was used to keep me warm *"cuando nos vayamos para el norte, "*—when we go north—as she called leaving for the United States. The cloth had been bartered for in the black market where my father had become an expert trader. Two chickens and some *yuca* had accompanied it. A trade for old ten-cent store jewelry that my mother had learned was a great bartering tool in the farmlands of Matanzas when dealing with the *campesinos* whose daughters were about to wed.

My skin itched from the cloth. It smelled bitter. It smelled of fear. Fear had been a constant companion of mine for many years by then. Fear that my father would be jailed for his clandestine fast-food kiosk secreted behind the house. Fear that my parents would be taken to La Cabaña where all the *gusanos* or "worms", as the communist called us, went when accused of being counterrevolutionaries. Mostly, fear that I would be the cause of their misfortune.

It had not been very long that a patrol car of the military police had driven over the same rugged road we now traveled and stopped to ask where I had bought the milk shake that I so recklessly drank unaware of the potentially disastrous consequences of my indiscretion. Fear was real. Fear was justified.

Fear was my constant companion. A companion that no eleven-year-old should have at his side constantly, or for so many years. But I knew that the man who sold milk shakes on Apodaca Street was Pepe Mena. My dad. Not only did he sell *batidos*, but also *papas rellenas*, *croquetas* and anything else he could concoct in our kitchen with what few spices and ingredients for which he could barter. *Carne rusa*, an Eastern Bloc version of Spam, inedible to most, became a delicious creation in my father's enterprising culinary hands. Soon these would be some of the lasting memories that I would carry to my new life in the United States.

These are the best recollections of a youth who grew into adulthood molded by two cultures. An example of growing up American as part of a generation lost whose identity is found in both and whose complete acceptance by either is denied him.

What is incontrovertible is that the United States of America opened its arms and took me to its bosom. Not having been born here, I chose to love this country. I served her when I felt I needed to repay her is some small measure for her kindness.

I respect her, stand in awe of her, and cherish every moment I've spent in her loving embrace.

CHAPTER 2

Exit Visas and
A Night of Anguish

In 1967, Blanca, my mother's half-sister who lived in Washington, D.C., sponsored our family to migrate to the U.S. under the Freedom Flights program. Our exit number had been frequently repeated when discussing the ones scheduled to leave Cuba on any given week. Ours was, 107,954. The exit number was our passage on the Freedom Flights to the United States. However, it was not uncommon to hear of deals being made by desperate parents who needed to have their teenage sons leave Cuba before the age of 15.

Fifteen was a pivotal point in a young man's life: the start of the compulsory military service that would prevent him from leaving Cuba until after age 27; if even then. Fifteen was also the birthday I would never celebrate in Cuba, "no matter what," my father used to say. My parents were determined that their oldest son was not going to be another casualty of Castro's exportation of communism to the rest of the world. We would leave, even if we had to leave by boat, *por lancha*, as most called it. Actually such an escape had been planned once before and resulted in the vilest form of betrayal of my father's trust.

Leaving by boat or raft was something with which I had also become intimately familiar by then. My 17-year-old maternal uncle, Antonio, and a close friend of the family, José Manuel, had been entrapped by a government informant who incited them into attempting an escape by raft that resulted in jail sentences for both in the Cuban political prison system.

Details were few. It was commonly known, however, that they had embarked outside of Cabo Francés in the Isle of Pines with the informant who lead them into a waiting Cuban patrol boat not too far from the coast. Antonio was jailed in Oriente province and later transferred to a Matanzas prison. José Manuel, whom I also considered an uncle, fared a much more malevolent fate in La Cabaña.

Fortunately, we did not have to exit by sea as many did. Our departure was less treacherous, albeit equally nerve wrecking. A departure toward a new beginning arranged by my father—bartered for as with the food for which he illegally traded—with a government official he met through Elena, a neighbor who dated the man. Even at eleven years old, I knew that as my father arranged for us to leave Cuba in order to save our family, it was at the expense of another.

CHAPTER 3

Varadero

Varadero had long been considered the most beautiful beach in the whole of Cuba, "no, in the whole world," insisted my uncle, Fermín, who, of course, had only known Cuban beaches. "Much nicer than El Mégano, Santa María or Cojimar," he would comment in his customary relaxed matter-of-fact style.

I had been there as a child with him. It had been an all-day affair. We had left early in the morning, before sunrise, and took the train to Matanzas. From there we walked over to the bus station and boarded the Varadero line. The bus ride was beautiful. I thought that Fermín was right about Varadero, but then again, I often agreed with him unquestionably.

The natural beauty of the landscape was captivating, even for a young child. I also remembered frolicking in Varadero's crystalline blue waters. Unlike El Mégano, where he used to take us often, or Santa María, where we also frequently swam, Varadero Beach was never deep. That was part of its beauty, I had been told. "You can walk out to the horizon and never go deeper than your waist," Fermín would assure me.

I also remembered the street traffic, and the clubhouse where we changed into our swimming trunks and later back to our street clothes. I thought the seashore's ornate wooden benches on the sand-covered streets were the most beautiful I had ever seen. These were my memories of Varadero. The images that would project in my mind whenever I thought of what I believed to be Cuba's most beautiful beach. This night, however, would be very different.

We arrived at sundown. In the twilight, I could still see people loitering outside the airport. Most said their goodbyes to friends, relatives—or in some cases—to parents who would remain behind with older boys of military age, or with other family members that had problems with their exit papers sacrificing themselves by remaining behind so that the rest of the family could know a life free from oppression.

The fashion in which my father had arranged our passage from communist Cuba did not guarantee more than the new exit documents; and these often had mistakes that would prevent the bearer from exiting the island. I was very much aware of the conditions of the arrangement, as I had witnessed its informal transaction on a sultry January night weeks earlier.

Dad's exit visa mistakenly showed his maternal surname as Cabrera, a common Spanish surname, rather than Cabreja, the very uncommon surname of my paternal grandmother's family. His passport said, Cabreja. The exit documents also showed the wrong maternal family name of the exit documents. It was anticipated that Cuban officials would discover the mistake during the inspection process prior to our departure and that we would have to make a decision: the entire family stay, or leave *papi* behind. To me the decision was obvious. However, as I later learned, what was not obvious to me was my parent's resolve that I would not serve in Castro's military.

These were the promptings of my friend, "Fear," as I traveled the streets of Varadero and earlier as I traversed the streets of my youth for the last time on my way there. My last recollections of the historic city of Guanabacoa, the only home I had known, were of grim faces standing street side watching the slow exodus from their midst. Raúl González, my friend, cried. So now did the many faces I did not know in Varadero. I wished to cry too. But I feared to do so.

CHAPTER 4

The Inventory

Just three days earlier, my brother Rafael and I had walked to school as usual. At about eleven in the morning the Director of our school, a short mulatto woman—a communist of convenience—and the aunt of Tomasito, one of my classmates, escorted a group of neighbors I knew well across the school grounds. Ana, Fermín's wife, walked behind the plump figure followed by a group of people whose faces I can see, but whose names or relationships have fallen from memory.

They moved with purpose and intent and walked into my classroom as if headed to engage in some important undertaking. Someone in the group spoke to me in a loud excited voice, "Come, my child, get your brother and come, you're leaving Cuba ... that's right, get your little brother, you're going North!" Their excitement was open—defiant even. Perhaps, because they did not realize that their excitement had forced into submission the usual fear of thought and expression that constantly accompanied Cubans in the adolescence of communism.

"Could it be?" I thought. "How would they know?"

"Hurry child, they've finished the inventory."

El inventario. It was true. Inventory was the point of no

return, the guarantee that your number was up. It was well-known that as soon as the government official completed the *inventario*, with its thorough cataloguing of all personal and real property of those who were leaving Cuba, a departure date would follow within days.

A revolutionary stalwart, accompanied by our neighborhood's head of the *Comité de la Defensa de la Revolución* performed the *inventario*. The CDR or Committee for the Defense of the Revolution was the neighborhood official government watchdog.

In our neighborhood, one where friendships were of greater value than loyalty to communism, even by staunch communists, the CDR chief was Felipe, a true friend and one of my father's best clients at the nocturnal, and very illegal, food stand. Felipe had always looked the other way. He was a simple man of humble beginnings and an even more humble station in life in adulthood.

His sons were our friends, his wife a nice lady. No one ever spoke ill of the quiet, small, black man who lived at the end of *calle Apodaca* by *Cadena* street across from the sandlot where impromptu baseball games would often take place. It was a place well-known to all. It was there—at the trash-ridden field—that our garbage was dumped into the communal tanks for later burning, or buried in the gully just behind the tanks. All manner of twisted metal and decomposing refuse could be found in this block-long parcel.

One of my few recollections of Felipe is of the night he came to our house and knocked on the side door. My father had just closed the stand. On the shortwave radio, we listened to the Spanish Service of the Voice of America my future employer many years later. My head rested on my dad's shoulder wrapped by his powerful and comforting arms. He listened intently to VOA every night hoping to catch a glimpse of life in the U.S. as Tomás Blacoutt and Pepe del Río would speak of snow-covered winter nights in Washington, D.C. Perhaps, he hoped, he would also hear a rerun of his favorite recording: *Celoso* by Marco Antonio Muñíz.

Many a night was spent dreaming of a future life as we listened to these familiar voices—aware of the risk of incarceration for listening to *Yankee propaganda* an indefensible counterrevolutionary act as far as Castro's government was concerned.

At the door, Felipe spoke in his usual soft voice and subdued demeanor. He wished to make it very clear to my father, he repeated, that what he asked was a favor. "It pains my heart," said Felipe, "my face falls from shame," he continued in the colorful and oft-overemotional Cuban vernacular because of what he was about to ask. "My kids have nothing to eat and I have no money with which to pay you, tonight," he timidly explained.

His honest admiration and respect for my father had long been established. The outlawed food stand had functioned since 1967 or 1968 and never had Felipe done anything but protect my father. My father was not only liked, but most important, he was respected. He was a humble man, the son of an Oriente tobacco farmer. He had chosen to live in a humble Guanabacoa neighborhood. Well below his means, but well within his people.

Memories still endure in my mind of other times in our neighborhood that earned him that respect. I recall my father, a rope around his waist, with Fermín or sometimes another man from the neighborhood at the other end, brave the gale winds of an approaching hurricane. They searched for friends whose houses were at peril during the storm. Our house was of better construction and more spacious then that of most of our neighbors, so it would serve as a refuge during the storm. What little we had would be shared and together—as neighbors—we would weather the passing of the tropical storm.

Felipe and his family had been among us many, many times. In fact, I can't think of anyone in the neighborhood who had not. "Come, don't be foolish," my father would plead. "I know your house is good, but why stay there by yourself?" he would contend with those reluctant to accept a helping hand, pride being a trait of the Cuban people. And when his powers of persuasion were at an end, he would finally appeal to their character, "besides, I need your help." Help he knew how to give. And he gave willingly and without reservation. This night, with Felipe, would be no exception.

"You know that your money is no good in my house," my father protested. "Aren't you my friend?" my father asked. Felipe stared at the floor. "So, this is not a payoff either, this is a friend who doesn't want his friend's children to go to bed hungry," my father reassured Felipe.

Our stove was lit and *croquetas* and *papas rellenas* were fried while the shimmering flames of the propane burners warmed bread. "This … I will never forget," Felipe promised, as he walked away with a large plate of food. A promise he kept. The food would be sufficient to feed his children, as well as himself and his wife. More important, it would be enough to mollify my father's sense of duty, assured in the knowledge that he had done yet another good deed because it was the right thing to do. My mother, already in bed, did not protest.

When Rafael and I got home from school, we learned that a complete listing had been taken of all of our worldly possessions. These had been catalogued and filed by the government official. Should any of these items be missing on the day of our departure, our exit visa would be negated and the possibility of imprisonment for those involved in "stealing the People's property" was equally real. El *inventario* had been completed.

It was here that Felipe kept his promise of loyalty to my father, as we learned nearly a year after having arrived in the United States. *Cuqui*, my father's nephew whom my dad had taken in years earlier with his wife, betrayed him.

Angry because my father did not reveal the whereabouts of the hidden dollars he left behind, my cousin filed a report with Felipe as head of the CDR denouncing my father's clandestine food stand and his black market dealings demanding justice and hoping to stop our departure from the island. Felipe promised to inform the proper authorities immediately, which he did, two days later.

On the evening of the *inventario*, my father was visited by his contact at the office coordinating the exit permits and told that we would be leaving the next day, or the day after, just as he had advised my father a week earlier to be ready to leave the following week. Leaving our native soil and starting our new life was only a few hours away.

It was then that my father made the arrangements to have my Uncle Fermín and his family to leave the island in another illicit transaction that would affect another family, while rescuing my uncle and my cousins from the oppressive situation we lived in our country at the time.

CHAPTER 5

Solidarity and Other Lies

I made telephone calls on the eve of our departure. I remember walking the long streets of Guanabacoa to a schoolmate's house. It was the first time that I had actually used that extravagant marvel that seemed to work by magical powers: the telephone. The joy of using the phone was greater, I think, than my excitement at leaving Cuba.

Teachers were notified of my departure, and in keeping with good deportment as well as in tribute to their assistance in my formation, each was personally thanked for having educated me. It was expected of me. I called *Señorita Alonso, Señorita Cira* and la *Señorita Directora.* The former two had been influential in my education, the latter was required.

That night, our house became a constant flow of visitors and well-wishers coming to pay their respects, say their goodbyes and show solidarity with our anti-communist feelings in the quietest of possible ways. In fact, the strongest oration on the ills of communism came from my fifth grade teacher, one we had long believed, beyond a doubt, to be a devout and fervent communist. But in communist Cuba, things are not always as they appear.

But that was yesterday. Tonight was another chapter as my parents, my maternal grandmother, my younger brother and I waited at the Varadero airport. As we prepared for our exodus, the tension built. Recollections of the day before seemed of little importance and light years away. This night, a long night, as it would turn to day, would become life changing. All would be affected, if not physically, psychologically. My father produced the documents that would grant us passage to the holding area where we would spend the next 12 to 14 hours. First stop was Cuban emigration.

Next, everyone was subjected to a perfunctory physical examination. All would suffer humiliation and degradation. As citizens of an oppressive society we were used to these indignities. The aspersion of the moment was spared to none.

Communism can be readily defined in its purest forms at these times. Everyone an equal, everyone reduced to the lowest form of communal misery. Communists, it seems, dispense equality in great measure whenever it is done to denigrate the human spirit. Equality of communism had made all Cubans, equally poor and equally miserable.

The representatives of Cuba's revolutionary government appropriated all matter of jewelry or anything of value. All there knew full well of this government sanctioned piracy perpetrated night after night. If it was of value, it remained behind in the hands of our oppressors. Value was defined in great part by the sentimental attachment to the item by the person departing the island. Photographs, letters, wedding bands, ornate handkerchiefs, if it held any emotional value it was confiscated by our "*comrades.*" My grandmother attempted to hold back a stream of tears.

A ring had been taken from her. It was a talisman of little actual value that she had worn from her youth, a gift from her father. Having been divested of most of our earthly goods already, there was little to take from us that night at the Varadero airport.

Most of my mother's jewelry had already been traded by my father for contraband in the black market. The few other valuables she possessed she had given to friends and family, a preferable fate to having been disposed of them at the hands of those whom we fled at the airport.

Our most treasured possessions, photographs of our family, had been left for safekeeping with Maria. She was a neighbor and my mother's best friend since mom married my father. She had been at our side for as long as I could remember. That friendship would endure until her death a decade later.

For my father, another valuable stayed behind, so precious that he seldom spoke of her for many years, and then only to me, my sister Marta, my father's only daughter.

My memories of her are of a chubby pig-tailed girl pushing me in the swing behind the house. My dad had asked her to come with us, but she chose to stay behind. Her mother, my father's first wife, a fervent supporter of Castro, found in the revolution the validation she never sought to otherwise have and did an exhaustive job of indoctrinating my older sister—Martica, as I still call her—into Marxism-Leninism.

Marta's last, well-rehearsed words to my father prior to his departure were, "If you really wanted to be my father, then you would choose the revolution. I cannot love a father who has abandoned the sacrifices of the revolution." Fortunately, the words of an adolescent pained by her father's departure, while tragic at the time, did not diminish his love for his child.

We sat in the well-lighted waiting area of the Varadero airport until after midnight. It was then that our names started to be called: "Acosta, Aragón, Bermudez" and so on. Young and old alike, we began to form a single line. "Manríquez, Medina, Mena." At the end of the line awaited a vaccination needle.

One by one we shared yet another icon of communist equality, a contaminated needle used on multiple individuals much in the same fashion cattle ranches inoculate multiple cattle with a single device.

The effects of the vaccine were well known to the exiled community. Three days of high fever caused by infection, while the spot of the vaccination would swell and blister leaving a scar to serve as a reminder of the last night in Castro's Cuba.

During the night, none spoke. Fear, again, permeated the night. Only a small child of about four or so would dare raise her voice. "*Si tú te vas al Coppelia, para comerte un helado ...,*" sang the tiny soloist, mimicking a popular song of the time. "I sing just like Luisa Maria Güell," she would proudly say. No one was a greater contributor to the preservation of sanity that night than young Cari.

I remained awake all night. My old companion— "Fear"—was close at my side again. My father and mother embraced, while Rafael slept on the chairs to my father's left, his head resting on my dad's lap. It is the remembrance of the horror of that night that makes me fume with ire at the slightest defense of Castro or of communism. It is not a political feeling. It is a pain that lives in the deepest confines of my soul that hates the memory of that night. And of those who caused it. Many times I have heard ignorant souls, paperback communists, who spouse liberal causes out of romantic ideals thinking they have a given knowledge of the altruistic works of communism and socialism. They speak with great authority about something of which they know little about. And what little they know is a filtered version of leftist ideals, far removed from the reality that we survived. I'm not sure that I really understand the concept of hatred. The reaction to the memories of that night would be my definition of it. It is as destructive a feeling as I can find.

The Cuban sun soon began to break the darkness of the night as night turned to day. It marked the new beginning for all us that February morning. For some, a beautiful new beginning full of promise and opportunities; for others, a dark moment never to be forgotten, nor to recover from its aftermath, its dark consequences to last an entire lifetime.

Freedom was just a few yards away. It waited in the passenger cabin of a transport aircraft on the runway of the Varadero airport. Forty minutes of flight and we would land in the Promised Land, 90 miles across the Florida Straits, due northeast to Miami International Airport. Two long tables were placed by the double glass doors that lead to the last footsteps on Cuban soil and to the inside of the airplane a short distance away. These tables served as the definitive tribunal of communist justice that would determine whether we lived as freemen or whether our family would be destroyed.

On the table nearest to the seats where we had waited all night, sat an American from the United States Interest Section. To us he was from the Swiss Embassy, since that's where the U.S. Interest Section was housed due the lack of formal diplomatic relations between Cuban and the United States at the time. Next to him, on the other table, sat a Cuban government official whose job was to find fault in any of the documents. Some were indeed found. The first casualty that morning was Cari's father. A young man still not quite thirty.

The murmuring of the crowd followed by the penetrating shriek of anguish vocalized by his young wife, served as evidence that one of us had fallen. Cubans are a people with a tremendous sense of kinship and of fair play. In different circumstances, perhaps, these Cuban officials would have had to answer to the protests of those who witnessed the destruction of the young family. But in the circumstances of the moment, they did not dare speak; they did not even dare to reflect on the injustice that was being perpetrated by those avowed defenders of Castro's revolution, lest they too should fall.

The man's maternal last name had been misspelled on the exit visa. A simple and very common mistake that would have been a source of laughter at any other time, but not here, too much was at stake. He pushed his grieving wife from his arms and cried out: "Someone, please hold on to her and my little girl. Please don't let them come back. Please, someone, please hold on to my wife. Make sure she gets to Miami with my little girl."

Cari screamed, *"Papi, mi papi. ¿Qué le pasa a mi papi?"*
Someone did wrestle the young woman from the broken

young man. Cari continued to wail, "What is happening to my daddy?" Two aged men, ahead in line and already cleared, took the woman in their arms and another carried Cari to the plane. My dad and another man held onto the young father as he shouted again, "Please take them to Miami, please take them! Don't let my wife and little girl come back." No one in line dared to say a word. Eyes were down and tears dropped silently onto the tiled floor. Two military policemen quickly arrived and grabbed the young man by an arm and lead him toward the exit. He had been cast into the abyss of communist bureaucracy.

Cari's and her mother's voices and their desperate anguish often cry out to me in the night. Their utterances have become intolerable sounds too painful for me to bear. Their sweet voices evoke the darkest and deepest pain in my being. The image of the young, tormented father being held back by his compatriots—his comrades in arms of that night—an image that I would remove from my mind's eye were it humanly possible.

Never, save on my parent's death, have I cried so wretched tears as I have over the years at the mere thought of Cari's dad and of his great oblation.

Just as quickly as it had begun, the scene ended and the government officials went back to work. The man reached out his hand for the papers of those next in line. My parents were numb. Just minutes later it was our turn. At the table the American diplomat immediately found the mistake on the Cuban government issued papers. My dad's demeanor reflected concern affected by the events witnessed minutes earlier. His voice quivered as he started to explain.

At seeing the panic in my father's eyes, the consular worker abruptly interrupted him. *"Bien. Adelante,"* he said, diverting attention from my father's documents. "You know," he told the Cuban official as he turned toward him. "I can't wait to get back home and see real baseball." Castro's man stopped and directed his attention at the American. "What?!" he responded disbelievingly. "Last night, *Industriales* and *Mineros,*" said the diplomat. "I could not even finish the game."

What ensued, by design, was an energetic debate about Cuban baseball versus the Major Leagues. In the importance given the exchange—since few things are more important to a Cuban than baseball—Castro's representative, defiantly defended the honor of our national players abandoning all interest in my father's papers. He then nonchalantly stamped all five exit visas without a glance, while continuing his vehement defense of *la pelota cubana.* The exchange faded as we hastened our stride toward the aircraft.

My father, as he later confessed to my mother, was so distraught that he was about to volunteer the mistake on the Cuban exit documents. I felt it was only because of divine intervention that my family was kept intact, unlike Cari's.

On the plane, I sat at the window seat to my mother's right and my father sat directly behind her with Ralph next to him. My grandmother sat across the aisle from my father. Not a single word was spoken during the ensuing twenty minutes that we waited. No one dared. We were almost free now. But the trepidation born of censorship through intimidation was still in effect. The plane eventually loaded its final passengers.

Contradicting emotions permeated the cabin. Anguish over the loss of Cari's father, over the misfortune that had transformed a beautiful, hopeful family into a calamity. There would not be a realization of dreams nor a hopeful, new beginning for them in the land of promise that awaited us.

Finally, my mother, who while addressing me spoke to all said: "Look out there children. This is your country. Remember it well, for I fear that you will never see it again." Silent tears accentuated our farewell to the island of our birth, the country we left behind.

CHAPTER 6

The Promised Land

Our new life began on February 11, 1969. The Freedom Flight touched down on the Miami runway to applause, cheers and tears of joy. Our emotions had been released from the bondage of communism. This was freedom, true freedom. The land of milk and honey for a people who only minutes earlier had witnessed the cruelty of a tyranny intent on crushing the human spirit.

One by one, we walked to the plane door. And one by one we stepped down to touch the hollowed soil of liberty. I walked ahead of my parents with my grandmother and Rafael. I took in the Miami Airport landscape. Abruptly, a reverent silence suddenly saturated the air. All movement had been brought to a halt. The cheers and sounds of exaltation verbalized by my compatriots silenced. I looked back to see what could have caused such a curt end to our revelry. My father and mother knelt on the ground and quietly lifted their voices to God thanking Him for our deliverance. It was a brief unrehearsed gesture, a reaction as unnatural in communism as logical in the land of freedom.

The moment was sweet and it was virtuous. It was potent with the elixir of religion and free speech. I was home. I had just met this exquisite beauty named, America. She was easy to love. She removed from me the burden of trepidation and allowed me to say goodbye, if for a moment, to my otherwise constant companion: Fear. She made my father and me free men. For some, perhaps it will be difficult to understand. But for those of us who experienced having the shackles of communism removed from our minds and from our bodies, it was a glorious exaltation of the soul. I looked at my parents, and could see in them an immediate change too. My grandmother crossed herself as she watched them kiss the ground and regain their place with the group.

All kinds of extemporaneous expressions of the joy we, the newly arrived, felt had been documented. Memorable moments shared by the exiled Cuban community often with some embellishment I'm sure.

The story tells about an incident on another flight. One of the last to step down from the plane was a blind man of about 25. He had been allowed to leave because of his infirmity. He had lost his sight only a couple of years earlier, as the story is told. During the long wait of the night before, he had sat quietly in a corner. An older woman, his mother it was assumed, had sat with him throughout the night. Now, as he was brought by the stewardesses to the top of the rolling stairs, he threw the cane onto the tarmac followed by his dark eyeglasses and let out a loud yell screaming for all to hear: *"Here, Fidel, these sunglasses are for you, you wretch!"*

Laughter and applause erupted. He had beaten the system. In him the indomitable human spirit was celebrated. Craftiness, another hallmark of the Cuban people lived in its truest form. He had played his charade, not to avoid the hard labor that my parents and hundreds of thousands of dissenters had been caused to endure. He had proposed to prove to Castro and his regime that they had been unable to take from us our legacy: our humor and our resourcefulness. We were Cubans, the sons and daughters of José Martí and Antonio Maceo, the children of the *Mambí* who armed with only machete and mettle, defeated Spain. The legacy of Carlos Manuel de Céspedes who on October the 10th of 1868 called every Cuban to lay down his life if necessary to abolish Spanish colonialism.

A new page had begun to be written in our histories. Its first entry said: "We are Cubans. We are both a reverent and an ingenious people. As Americans we will base our character on this foundation."

CHAPTER 7

Miller High Life,
Big League Baseball and Ham

Assembled once again in a large waiting room, we awaited an interview by American immigration officials. The first glimpse of the United States was a visual feast. Some of the immigration workers had at their desks chocolate bars: Milky Way, Snickers and Hershey bars, the brown sleeve covering the aluminum foil that surrounded the incredibly beautiful partially eaten chocolate of the latter taunted us.

This was America, the land of plenty. Others chewed gum, what every American chewed night and day. Everyone knew that. Another well-known fact was that Americans were all blond and drove only new cars and that they ate a whole meal for breakfast and almost nothing for lunch. And they drank Coca Cola, Pepsi Cola, every imaginable type of cola known to mankind. I observed in wonderment. I could hardly wait to taste them all.

There was much to savor in my new country: Miller High Life, Chesterfields, Cadillac, Chevrolet, Gillette razors, and ham, lots of ham. These were the things that obsessed most Cubans longing for a time before the revolution or migrating to the United States. Hours were spent reminiscing about these things they no longer had but hoped to have once they arrived in U.S. I too longed for these things, even though I did not shave, smoke, drive nor did I remember the taste of ham. They seemed important to everybody else, so I too had developed an affinity for these things.

Perhaps, Miller High Life was sweet. It had to be; otherwise, it would not taste right, like the sip of Cuban beer I had stolen from my uncle when he had been allowed to purchase a few bottles for a birthday party.

During special occasions, such as weddings, the government would, upon proper documentation having been produced, issue a special allotment of beer and soft drinks. If these items were available, then one could be allowed to have a meagerly sample at least once a year.

Miller had to be sweet. Everything in America was sweet. And there was plenty of it. And baseball. Not just any type of baseball: big league baseball. Mickey Mantle, Yogi Berra, Babe Ruth and Lou Gehrig. Maybe I could see them play. I had heard much about them from my father and his friends. How old were they?

How could so much talent be gathered in one team? Surely the Yankees had not lost a game ever; not even to the fabulous Saint Louis Cardinals. I was a Yankees fan. I had never seen them play, but my father said that they were the best. The big leagues had Cuban players too: Camilo Pascual, Mike Cuellar, Mini Miñoso and, Dagoberto Campaneris. Maybe there was room for one more Cuban in the bigs. "I would choose to play for the Yankees," I had repeatedly informed my dad. They were my team. I could hardly wait to see them play.

As we waited, my mind had almost magically transformed into the mind of a child again. Gone, I thought—not knowing that old friends stay with you forever—was fear. I was rid of the dread attached to every action of my being. I was free to think. Free to let my mind wander without reservation. Could this be freedom? I asked myself.

At first, the man behind the desk examined the documents. I knew that they would find the mistake on my father's papers, but it made no difference this time. Well, actually, it did. After completing the first phase of the immigration interview, my father was taken to another room.

"Didn't they catch it? The man asked. "No," said my father. It just did not make sense. No one made it out with such a mistake, unless, of course, they were Castro's plants sent by the communist government to spy on the Cuban community in exile.

Further inquiry was needed. While we waited, little boxes were passed to all. They contained gum, juice and HAM SANDWICHES! Wow, it was true. Everyone ate ham for breakfast, lunch and dinner. I had eaten ham before. I could not remember it, but I had been one of the fortunate few I'd been told—the last of the ham generation.

It was spoken of as if it were the wearing of a badge of honor. "*Jamón, ¡claro!*" Of course I had tasted ham. I was the legacy of pre-communist Cuba. I had tasted ham as a child. It made me special somehow.

I reasoned that Cuban ham from before the revolution tasted different. It was not quite as.... well ... as American tasting. Besides, this one did not taste the same because of the mustard. It would take some getting used to it again, I thought. I'm just out of practice of eating ham that was all.

Lunch concluded and we still awaited the return of Papi from what my grandma, *"Abue,"* feared was an interrogation. "Questioning," I emphatically told my grandma. Interrogations were commonplace in Cuba; "They don't have them here," I assured her.

None of us actually knew that it really was an interrogation. We just assumed that it was all part of the process. The interview, as the immigration agents referred to this interrogatory, lasted the better part of four hours. My father was asked about all sorts of political questions. Whether he had affiliations with this group or that group. Later, they attempted a ruse: "We know for a fact, José, that you are a member of Cuban intelligence." He laughed, he told us later. "If you cooperate, we'll let you and your family stay."

My father knew it to be a ruse and never doubted for a minute that we would be allowed to stay. God meant it that way, he said. If the Cuban's had not stopped his exit, the Americans would not deport him. This was the land of liberty and he had earned the right to be here. In as far as anti-communists went my daddy was the biggest of them all. Not to mention that, aside from his dislike of communism, he was the only Cuban known to me who actually subscribed to an apolitical disposition. In the overall scheme of things, the questioning was just a minor inconvenience.

Satisfied that my father was not a communist agent of Castro's regime, we rejoined the rest of our group at the Freedom House. *La Casa de la Libertad* was a unique and exquisite place to make the transition. We got there in time for dinner. Again, there was lots of food and almost anything we wanted to drink. My father was given 25 U.S. dollars. Some of the money was immediately used to purchase gum and candy for my brother and me. My father smoked a pack of Chesterfields. I chewed on Wrigley's double-mint gum with reckless abandon, although the taste of mint has prior to and since been intolerable for me. But for those two days at Freedom House, even mint tasted pleasurable.

CHAPTER 8

Old Wounds in a New land

During our brief stay in Miami, we visited old acquaintances that had managed to come before us. One of them was Emilio. It saddens me that I cannot remember his last name. He was a kind man. I had liked him from the first time that I had met him. He loved my grandmother. My grandmother, Caridad, whom I lovingly called Abue was 58 years old at the time and the best friend a child ever had. She and Emilio had been an item for most of my life. He was soft-spoken and kind. He was a considerate man who loved my grandmother and her family. We all reciprocated his love. He never bought our love, nor had he attempted to. His demeanor and the gentleness of his being made us wish that my grandmother would make him a permanent part of her life. She loved him too. I had asked many times why she had not married him? "Ay, Papo. I'm much too old for that, baby."

Abue was fiercely independent. She had married my grandfather at age 14. By fifteen, my uncle Fermín had been born. Two years later, my mother Regla Jorge Hernándes had entered this world as well. Abue longed for freedom all her life. She quickly divorced the old sergeant, Fermín Jorge Gil, and returned to Casablanca by Havana harbor where she had been raised. The children were placed in her mother's care. It was the beginning of an unhappy childhood for her children and the beginning of the insecurity that characterized my mother's life until the day she died.

My grandmother became an unfashionably independent woman, working, dancing, traveling, while her children were shuttled between Casablanca and the small town of Cidra in Matanzas, the province directly east of Havana. The Old Sergeant or *Papaucha*, as we called him was short, fat and carefree. A Havano cigar was never far from his lips. He had been a sergeant in the Cuban Army in Cidra years prior to the revolution, which had entitled him to certain privileges. Among them was that of running a small general store from his house. Prior to the revolution and for a short time thereafter prices were fair and products plentiful. Trouble was never present. In his spacious home, he also kept a small office. In it was an old, large roll-top desk.

Many a time as a child I had rummaged through those desk drawers. They contained many wonders. Photographs of clowns, acrobats, soldiers, relatives and of my grandfather as a youth. In it were also photographs of my mother and Fermín. They had yellowed with time. In the middle drawer was the magic wand that he always brought out to perform tricks for the grandkids when we visited, which was not often enough. In a large wooden chest—just out of reach, above the desk— was Bartolo. A ventriloquist's dummy that had fascinated me from the first time he had spoken. I guess that this desk held all that was dear to my grandfather. He knew that I would explore through his desk, but he never forbade it. Perhaps, it was a museum of sorts that he wanted us to discover.

As a child I liked my grandfather, later in life, I grew to love him. He was a man to be admired. He was a descendant of European Jews who had migrated to the Canary Islands prior to moving on to Cuba. His fair complexion and soft, straight hair reflected the European blood that ran through his veins. As a child, he had literally run away with the circus. He had learned the trade of a magician and developed his ventriloquism. The details of that part of his life are sketchy in my recollection. I wish that I could remember more.

I saw him last in Cuba when I was only ten. Then, in 1983 he was granted a special visa to visit the United States and we resumed our friendship on the telephone. He had been very ill for many years. He had lived among people with grave diseases in San Lázaro on the western province of Pinar del Río. It was a long and closely held family secret and the exact illness never disclosed.

During his visit to the U.S. we spoke at length on the phone. He spent time in California during a short visit with my parents and my uncle Fermín. His voice sounded cheerful and filled with contentment. He said, "I am so happy to have been here with my children and to be able to talk with you kids, that I could just die right now without regret."

His words turned out to be prophetic. While spending a few days in Miami with my aunt Blanca after his California visit, he fell ill and quickly died. He is buried there.

Abue and he had become friends over the years. At the time of his death all bitter feelings had dissipated.

Unlike the bitter feelings my mother harbored for my grandmother most of her life and that while somewhat diminished, were not forgotten.

My mother had grown up without her mother. Her grandmother had been the only maternal influence in her life. She loved Reglita and how Reglita loved her. The petite blonde girl in the photographs had been raised by a kind, giving woman whom all called *mamá*. She had long been separated from her husband, my maternal great- grandfather, Francisco Hernándes. She raised her children and grandchildren alone and died relatively young.

And so, Reglita and Fermincito lived a harsh and cruel life traveling between Casablanca and Cidra. My grandfather remarried. Calixta Izquierdo, a young country girl from Matanzas who became my mother's and uncle's stepmother.

She was not much older than they were. She believed in physical punishment as a form of character development. My uncle believed in the same, so he often reciprocated after my mother had been beaten, correcting his stepmother's own lack of character. Without fail, every exchange of disciplinarian tactic by stepmother to stepchild, or stepchild to stepmother, was followed by a hurried exit from the Matanzas countryside to Havana by my young uncle with his little sister in tow. And without fail, each time, the old Sergeant would instruct that the children be returned. An easygoing soul, he never meted out punishment. There were no reprisals; however, Calixta was never happy to see them back. Eventually, both my mother and uncle would remain in Casablanca and grow up there.

Now, as we arrived in United States, my mother's ill feelings for my grandmother were very much alive. During my childhood, I had never heard them exchange any kind words. In fact, very few words at all.

My parents openly discussed whether my grandmother would stay in Miami with Emilio. Emilio wanted her at his side. He had rented a small apartment on the outskirts of Hialeah, not very far from the Miami airport. By my grandmother's own account, Emilio asked her to stay in Miami and marry him. She declined. He would be the only family that she would have had, had she chosen to stay in Florida. This was a new beginning for her too and she could not bear to be away from the company of her two grandsons, her dear son-in-law and, somewhat reluctantly, also her daughter.

Perhaps in this strange land, in the middle of a renaissance of spirit and mind for all of us, my mother would soften her heart and learn to forgive, or so hoped Abue.

CHAPTER 9

The Fable of Sunless Skies
And Other Tall Tales

Our stay in Miami was brief. Aside from the few visits we made to old neighbors and to distant relatives who had lived in the United States for some years, our time was spent in the confines of La Casa de la Libertad.

My father received five National Airlines tickets from the travel coordinator at the Freedom House. Since our final destination would be Washington, D.C., we were taken to a warehouse of sorts at the back of the Freedom House and there fitted with coats, gloves, hats and scarfs.

"Why are you guys going to Washington?" our compatriot asked. "Do you know how cold it is up there?" And in true Cuban style, pontification based on perception more than fact, said, "You guys might as well look at the sun for the last time, here. Up there the sun does not come out until the summertime, so, you better take as much sun as you can," said the woman outfitting us. She knew about these things. She had a sister who had once lived in Chicago. "Oh, but she lives in Miami now," she added. "Who can live in darkness for eight months out of the year?"

This would be the first of many such tales by people who freely gave their unsolicited opinion—ignorant observations that we later found to be based on a perverted sense of self-importance. We were newcomers. They were not. Thus, they knew all that there was to know about our new country and were more than happy to share it. To me the concept of living in darkness, as I visualized it, was a great concept; it meant snow and a veritable winter wonderland. I had watched many Canadian films at the Seventh-day Adventist Church that I had frequented clandestinely as a child. It would not be a bad thing. My parents, on the other hand, while somewhat skeptical of the description of the city that would be our home in our adopted land, feared that perhaps a slight bit of truth was to be found in these outrageous descriptions.

"Well, if it is true, we'll move to Tampa," my mother reassured my father. This was the magnificence of this country: change, boundless opportunities for anyone who dared to live life with its many challenges viewed as possibilities. My father agreed. Besides, my aunt, Blanca had lived in Washington D.C for almost five years, and she had made no mention of these cataclysmic conditions that had been described to us. Julián, Cora and the kids lived nearby in Virginia and they too seemed to be happy. If Washington D.C was as bad as we had been told, we could always move away to Virginia.

Coralia, or Cora, is my mother's adopted youngest sister. She is the daughter of Calixta's sister Esperanza. Esperanza had become mentally ill as a young adult and eventually took her own life. Calixta raised Cora. My mother had watched her grow at her side. Later in their lives, Calixta, Fermín and my mom grew to accept, at first, respect, later on, and eventually love one another. Coralia had become my mother's younger sister and they always referred to each other as such: *mi hermana.*

During her adolescence, Cora had lived with us in Havana. She had been sent there to keep her distant from a young man with little education and lots of charm, Julián González. He came from a poor peasant family of *"isleños"* from the Canary Islands. It was a large family, hardworking and engaging. The separation and distance was of no avail. Eventually they married and started their family. Cora, Julián and their three oldest children had followed Blanquita to the United States two years ahead of us.

Blanquita, in her late twenties, had recently remarried, this time in the U.S. to another Cuban immigrant whom she had met in Takoma Park, Maryland. She was a short, plump woman with long black hair and alert eyes. She was spirited and industrious, as much as she was fanatically dedicated to the Seventh-day Adventist faith.

She and my mother had a wonderful relationship and always loved each other without distinction of the fact that they only shared the same father. In a few short hours, they would be together again as we started our new life. With a resolve that we would not alter our plans, we were driven to the Miami airport.

Our coats close at hand and all of our belongings under the canopy of heaven stowed away in my mother's handbag; including forty-seven dollars; the twenty-five given my father and gifts from family and friends. This would be our first step on the road to becoming real Americans.

The flight would last just a little over two-and- a-half hours. We left Miami at dusk.

My mother looked deeply at the sun with nostalgic glee. Perchance the words of her countrymen were true. If so, perhaps, she thought, I may not see this wonderful orb of warmth for several months.

Our plane landed at Washington's National Airport just after eight thirty. The flight had been uneventful, except for our reluctance, at first, to accept the complimentary meal on the plane. Surely it would be expensive and we had very little money. Anxiety grew as we were given the food without asking. Everyone else had also been given food, "perhaps," my father said, "it would be impolite to turn the food away. We'll eat and let things sort themselves out later." We were finally put at ease, when one of the stewardesses, upon offering us a drink, said, "It's okay...they're free." Luckily, my mother, our interpreter with only limited means of communication, understood. She quickly alleviated our fears.

What a marvelous scene. Buildings tall and beautiful, bigger than any I had seen, aglow with glorious displays of light. The Washington Monument, the Jefferson Monument, the Reflective Pool. The glittering lights of the Watergate Hotel juxtaposed against the glittering blackness of the Potomac River greeted us with sublime enchantment. This was home now. And I liked it. I liked it very much.

It was a wonderful culmination to a trip that had started three days earlier on the streets of Guanabacoa. English! I would have to learn English! I always wanted to. I knew a few words, I told myself. Words from those books filled with pictures that my mother had kept from her trip to the U.S. after World War II. She had visited Miami and Tampa with a girlfriend. They had taken a cruise and visited the land of dreams, now, our home—forever.

CHAPTER 10

The Tobacco Farmer's Son

Life in Washington, D.C. was a challenge at first, especially for my father. Jose Mena Cabreja was born on October 10, 1924 in the small town of Sagua de Tánamo in the easternmost province of Oriente. He was the third youngest in a family of eleven children. "Fourteen children in total," he would explain lest one think he'd forgotten about the three that died in infancy.

His parents were the son and daughter of immigrants from the Canary Islands, Spain on his father's side, and from the Soria region of Spain and northwest region of France on my grandmother's side.

In Cuba they were landowners. They grew tobacco and their children's lives revolved around the splendid green sea of leaves that eventually would become the cigars for which the island is known.

From just before dawn to sunset they toiled the earth. Schooling was of lesser importance. Most of my father's generation attended until the second or third grade. Second grade was the sum of my dad's total formal education.

He was a kind, gentle man who was well-liked by most. His success with the ladies was "legendary" his brother, Domingo once told me. His charming simplicity always made him stand out.

Although poorly educated, he had a keen mind predisposed to quickly absorbing mathematics and complex machinery.

At 16 my dad decided the time had come to leave home and head for the bright lights of Havana. There he thought that he would make a life for himself. His father was not pleased with the decision. My dad left with one promise: there would always be a place for him at the table from the time of his departure, but he would not be allowed back home; my grandfather did not tolerate failure. This not so gentle prodding was to serve as a motivating force in my father's early life.

He arrived in Havana proper at the home of a maternal uncle who was a partner in a textile factory. There, my father was offered an apprenticeship as a textile mechanic. His income would be: room and board, a one-time advance for a new pair of dress shoes and a suit, and a meager salary with which he could just barely afford cigarettes and one or two meals a day. Happenstance, as it turned out, produced one of Cuba's top textile minds.

In the late 40's he met a young city girl in Havana named, Lázara. The details of their meeting, the ensuing romance that lead to their marriage and the birth of my sister, Marta, are little known to me and I never probed out of respect for my mother. What I do know is that life in Havana was difficult for them for many years.

Eventually, he gathered enough courage and confidence to leave his apprenticeship. Within a few short years he had become a prominent textile mechanic with an eye for developing new textiles and the machinery to weave it. His expertise as a mechanic was very much in demand and his ideas on machinery design had propelled him to some prominence.

By 1959, the year that the revolution overthrew Fulgencio Batista's government, he had married again and I was two years old. He had also successfully established a textile factory with his friend Leo in Guanabacoa. New machine components that he had designed started to arrive in crates to the factory in 1961 from North Carolina and New Jersey. Everything was received and accounted for, except for a key module that had been shipped separately to our house on Calle Apodaca due to its fragile nature and without which the new machinery would not work.

By this time, the Castro regime had nationalized much of Cuba's industry. Among those affected was my father. The actions that followed in early 1967 were more a declaration of emancipation from government abuse, than a political statement on his part. On top of our house were two water tanks constructed of concrete. These served as reservoirs for emergency use on a gravity-fed system. Late one night, shortly after the arrival of the aforementioned parts, he went to the reservoirs easily accessed by stairs designed to reach the roof much in the manner of a two-story building walk-up.

During the night, he drained one of the tanks and over the next few nights, my father could be found on the roof, building a false bottom to the reservoir and later depositing axle grease in sufficient amount as to cover the machine parts that had arrived at the house and that became of great interest to the Cuban government.

Once securely deposited in this vault that still holds them, my father built a watertight chamber and upon it poured a new false bottom ensuring that the components would not be damaged. Weeks later, our home was the subject of many thorough searches for these parts. Even our back yard was excavated in a futile search for the costly equipment.

My father's denial of ever having received these machine parts is the only time that I can think of him being dishonest. His honesty and sincerity were a distinctive trait of who he was. To me, it represents my father's unconquerable spirit of justice, independence and ingenuity. It also resulted in his being sent to labor camps.

CHAPTER 11

Maple Street

The drive to 6980 Maple Street was a visual feast and an attack on the senses. The effect of the car heater made me nauseous. Nerves contributed to it as much as the effect of the hot air on my face for the very first time. There were bright lights all around us as we drove the streets of Washington, D.C. across the Potomac River, over the 14th Street Bridge, by the White House and up 16th Street to Georgia Avenue. As we drove, Eliezer, my aunt's new husband recounted the tragic events of months earlier, the race riots provoked by the death of Martin Luther King.

I had heard about racism. Communist propaganda expounded repeatedly on what happened to blacks in the United States—especially Cuban blacks—"dogs are used to intimidate those of the black race that dare to speak against white injustice. Cuban blacks are especially despised, not only for being black, but for being foreigners as well," government-run *Radio Rebelde* would say.

Racism was a concept that I had a difficult time understanding.

"So blacks are hated, here?" I asked.

"Oh, no, not at all," said my aunt. "The mayor of

Washington D.C. is black. His name is Walter Washington. It is just that racism and politics intertwine sometimes, and this was a reaction to a sad event," she explained.

The fire damage to shops in the brownstone-lined streets of our nation's capital was visible even in the darkness of night. Painted slogans that I could not understand also marred the remains of what once had been places of commerce.

How could racism exist, at least as I understood it? Whites oppressing blacks, and yet, the governor ... mayor ... or president...whatever this man was, was black. There was much to learn.

Perhaps, there were cities with more blacks than whites where the blacks governed and in others, where whites were greater in number, whites were in charge, I reasoned. Maybe that was it.

My confusion grew even more when I distinctly heard Blanca's husband telling us to lock the doors and "be careful because the blacks are dangerous in Washington." Definitely. There was much to learn... especially English.

"Do kids speak English or Spanish, here?" I asked my aunt.

"English, of course," she answered.

"Even the babies," I continued.

"Yes. Even babies," she smiled.

As we drove, I thought about how this was the end of our trek. Our new home was here, and it would remain so, I said to myself. As the '69 Mercury Cougar traversed the snow and rain covered slick D.C. streets, I suddenly began to fear the unknown.

The excitement of the trip had reached a climax. Now, we were at journey's end. How long before I would be able to communicate? What would school be like? My friend, Fear, was again at my side.

Our destination was a three-story brown brick building with a basement, literally half a block from the Maryland state line. We parked curbside and walked into the building. It was dimly lit. We ascended the three flights of stairs to Aunt Blanquita's apartment at No. 5, 6980 Maple Street N.W., Washington, D.C. for the first time.

It was a spacious two-bedroom apartment. It was tastefully decorated with an unassuming layout. The living room had a small sofa bed that would serve as my brother's and my bed for the next few weeks. There was a rawhide stool with a longhorn etching on it. A record player console rested against the wall leading to the stairs on the other side, just to the right of the door. In it were several Cuban records, as well as a Jimmy Dean album, Adventist music and a Tennessee Ernie Ford 45 rpm.

My aunt had lived in this building for several years. She worked at the Adventist press just down the street on Carroll Avenue. Takoma Park, Maryland was to the Adventist as Salt Lake is to us Latter-day Saints. This was important to my aunt, a devout Seventh-day Adventist. My mother too had been a Seventh-day Adventist in Cuba. Religion had been a source of much contention among my parents. It had also been a refuge for my mother and me. Pastor Palacios, our minister, his wife and many of the congregation in Guanabacoa, had risked severe punishment for practicing their religion.

I remember walking at my mother's side on Máximo Gómez Street in Guanabacoa past *El Águila* bakery, more than three miles from our house, with a hymnbook wrapped in newspaper and a Bible likewise disguised— the red coloring on the edges of the pages diluted with alcohol and scraped off with a razor blade to give it the appearance of a textbook. Owning a Bible and hymnbook were *prima facie* evidence of *anti-revolutionary* activity.

Religion always played an important role in my mother's life. It was a keystone in mine, too. There at the old Spanish-colonial home where the Palacio family resided, we could be found worshiping most every Saturday. The living room had been converted into a chapel complete with rostrum and pastor's pew. Great tales of miracles and trials of faith fortified our own. Joyous strains of Protestant hymns were singing with vigor and spiritual outpouring during these meetings.

Worship services of praise fed the souls of a people unwilling to forget their duty to God and not wishing to forego His blessings in this difficult place and time. While the services were held, a young man would sit outside on the porch keeping a vigil for patrol cars. I am convinced, however, that the local authorities knew the existence of the meeting place and its growing membership. I am also convinced that, perhaps, a small lingering fear of their Maker prompted them to turn a convenient eye.

Adventist were not a direct and clear threat to communism—at least, not as much as the Jehovah's Witnesses because of their steadfast believes in pacifism as conscientious objectors. These fellow Christians were routinely persecuted, jailed and many killed in political prisons. They, however, were not the only ones, although probably the most persecuted that I knew.

Cuban jails during Castro's regime have been filled with religious martyrs who have laid down their lives rather than renounce their faith.

Accounts by political prisoners such as Armando Valladares and others attest to the ultimate trial of faith and the price paid by many Cubans of faith.

Being able to worship freely was a benefit of freedom never to be taken for granted by us. My mother, always in search of truth and light, a life-long quest, longed to hear the strains of hymns again. She wished to return to her church.

Months prior to our departure from the island, my mother had been excommunicated by the elders of the church for her failure to pay tithing on my father's meagerly income derived from the black market. When it was proposed by them that she leave my father whose atheist and belligerent attitude towards religion was harming our family and her spiritual growth, as they saw it, she refused; thus, her excommunication. Now, perhaps, she could make her case heard and she would be allowed back into the flock. That would be addressed in the coming days, but this night, our first night in Washington was marvelous.

As if scripted, our fondest wish had come true—at least for my brother and me. The crisp Washington D.C. skies turned light with snowflakes. We watched from the upstairs windows, our noses pressed against the cold glass. At first, the dark grass below us began to change colors.

The hollies and other shrubs around us glistened and eventually turned white. The reflection of the falling shapes against the streetlights excited us with an emotion seldom felt since.

"Grab your gloves and your scarfs," my mother said.

"You mean we can go out?" asked my younger brother, astonished that such a thing was even possible.

"Cover your ears, now," shouted my mom as we ran down the stairs.

It was cold, but the cold just served to awaken our senses. I would catch the falling flakes on my tongue.

"Don't do that, you'll get sick," my mother exclaimed. "It tastes like ice-cream," I joked.

Ralph learned how to make a snow angel from Eliezer, while my father watched gleefully. My aunt watched from the living room window above us. It was befit of a Norman Rockwell painting.

Photographs of that night still rank equal in importance to those of the births of my six boys. It was a splendid first night.

CHAPTER 12

A Rich Poor Family

"Are you sure?" my father asked. "I don't know how to repay you, but I know that I will," he said. It was February 14, 1969. It was a bitterly cold morning. It was also a great morning. Eliezer had found my father a job working construction with him. Today, they would be doing outside work. Suffering a high fever from the effects of the vaccine at the Varadero airport did not deter him.

He came here to provide a better life for his children. Nothing would keep him from capitalizing on an opportunity to work and provide for his family. It was just after 5:30 a.m. He kissed my mother goodbye as he walked out the door. He carried three dollars in his pocket, "for an emergency." He did not eat breakfast or lunch that day, nor the next. Dad did not want to spend the money. He would eat at night. It would be a good meal, so no need to concern himself with lunch, he thought. It was ironic, that the swelling of the shoulders that had plagued him while working in Castro's sugar-cane fields had disappeared—even in the frigid Washington winter.

Although ill from the effects of the vaccine, my father was happy and excited about working.

He had been employed one whole day. They would

not need him the following week, but he had tasted his first sip of the American Dream and of the opportunities that this country would offer his family.

At day's close, he asked his employer for an advance. His pay had been $14.00, after taxes, whatever that meant. He was late in coming home that night. About an hour late, but his reasons were good.

As he walked through the door he held in his arms a large box wrapped with silver paper and a white bow. This was Valentine's Day and he would not be remiss in celebrating his love for his wife. Inside the box was to be found a large doll of about three feet. "If you take me by the hand, I'll walk with you" the caption on the box said. It too was a magnificent moment in our lives.

The doll resided in my mother's bedroom until her passing. "My daughter," my mom would say when referring to it, only half-jokingly. Decades later, the depredations of time and the not so gentle hands of small children were evident in her less than perfect condition. Yet, the doll still wore the outfits that my mother has sewn for her over the years.

My father now knew that work could be found. So as soon as possible, we would look for an apartment. My aunt said that she would take us to the welfare office, so that we could be given the money to rent our own place. The concept of welfare was difficult for all of us to understand.

"It is not a hand-out," she insisted

"But, I can pay it back?" asked my father.

"I don't know, but the point is that you don't have to," continued my aunt.

"Well, we'll take it, but only if we can pay it back," he said.

My aunt agreed. Social Services gave my father $98 for the deposit and a like amount for the first month's rent. We would receive $238 a month for as long as we needed it, said the social worker. "You'll also get food-stamps you can use to buy groceries at the store," she added.

We were now well on our way to establishing our independence in our new country. The manager at the Long Branch Apartments showed us two or three apartments in the complex. Number eight at 8702 Gilbert Place, Takoma Park, Maryland, was chosen by my mother. It was clean and bright. It was not as spacious as our aunt's, but it was ours and it would suffice for our needs. It was a two-bedroom apartment on the third floor.

Long Branch Apartments were a happy mix of newly arrived immigrant families and lower income families who, in their majority, had relocated from southern states looking for work and a better way of life. We had that in common. It was a small complex of red brick apartments with a collection of families as different in culture, language and perception of their place in the world as one could find. To me, to my brother, to my grandmother, to my mother and to my father it was our new home.

CHAPTER 13

Returning to the Flock

Our first encounter with the Seventh-day Adventists in Maryland took place on the first Saturday of our new life. My aunt drove us to a meetinghouse on Aspen Road near the D.C. border. Eliezer would not participate; however, my father did accompany us. It was a large assembly hall with an ornate pipe organ that called out to Heaven itself. The pulpit was of gargantuan proportions in my young mind. The church even had a microphone. The Lord himself would be proud of this house of worship, I thought almost aloud. The congregation was "as great as the sands of the seas of which the Bible speaks," I remarked to my mother.

The Spanish-speaking pastor wore a fine suit and spoke words, both elegant and inspiring.

We prayed, we sang and we worshiped with the faithful. A few days later, a council was held regarding my mother. Nonetheless, because of her defiance of the elders in Cuba, my mother would still not be allowed back in the flock. "Perhaps," she said, "there is another Church out there that will take me." Her departure from the Adventist faith disheartened her, but never did she utter a bitter or demeaning word against them.

I too, still hold a special place in my heart for my Adventist brothers and sisters with whom I grew up in my native Cuba. Many of my most pleasant childhood memories are of these fine people whom I have not seen in over five decades. They instilled in me a deep sense of fairness, of fidelity and devout feelings of religious worship that have served me well throughout my life.

The Adventist social services did not turn their backs on us. Mainly because of my aunt and an old friend of the family, Carlos Cabrera, were influential in the church. Through them we were able to obtain some of the basics we needed to furnish our new apartment. From them we also received an old sofa with matching chair, a coffee table, dining table, four chairs, kitchen utensils, towels, sheets, two single beds and the mattress where my parents would sleep for the next year. The old discarded furniture could have not been more welcome anywhere else than in our new home.

A major first step had been taken. We were almost completely independent. We had our own place in our adoptive land. The future awaited our next move.

CHAPTER 14

Floating Pacifiers and
Other Marvels

Nearly ten days had passed since our arrival to the United
States. By now all of us had experienced the ill effects of
the vaccine from our last night in Cuba. One by one,
almost simultaneously, we had fallen with high fever and
convulsions. I was the last to suffer the consequences of
the contaminated needle. The redness of the spot in my
arm had turned into a blister about one inch in diameter.
Being bedridden as a result of the vaccine was a rite of
passage for the exiled Cubans.

Another rite of passage, at least for my friends and me,
was to put to the test the machinations and exaggerations
about the great miracles of American technology that ran
rampant in Cuba. Baby pacifiers in the United States
would float on air, preventing the nipple from touching
the floor. Coca-Cola would magically turn cold
immediately after removing the bottle cap. There were
machines that made sandwiches. All you needed to do was
insert the coins and select the type of sandwich you liked.
These were some of the apocryphal products known to
many of us. Just as the fact that all Americans were blond
and blue-eyed and that cars were disposable and that

everyone drove only brand new vehicles.

One of the miracles of American technology first discovered by me was frozen orange juice. During my vaccine-produced sickness, I was left behind at my aunt's house while she and my mother went grocery shopping. My fever had dissipated somewhat, so I could be left alone for an hour or two. A note left on the table read: "There is frozen juice in the freezer, drink some of it. Hope you feel better. Blanquita." Thirst from the fever required that I drink lots of fluids. Orange juice would hit the spot.

I took the Bird's Eye frozen concentrate and placed it on the table to defrost. Being a fan of *durofrios*, frozen juice cubes, I thought that a frozen treat would not only soothe my fever, but provide a tasty treat as well. Without hesitation, I proceeded to eat spoonful after spoonful of the tart indulgence. It required some getting used to, but, in general, it tasted rather good.

Later that evening, as we prepared to dine, my aunt asked where I had put the rest of the juice.

"You didn't drink all that juice, did you?" "Yes, it was only a can," I replied.

"You mean, you didn't mix it with water?" she asked half-jokingly, half concerned.

"No, I ate it with a spoon ... like *durofrio*," I answered fearful that I would be viewed as a glutton.

She called my mother into the kitchen and laughingly explained to her what I had done. I felt somewhat ridiculed, but justified in my ignorance.

Speculation about my physical wellbeing was openly discussed. What would the result be? "He will probably suffer from diarrhea," my mother suggested. "Probably," Blanquita said. As it happened, the opposite was true and eventually I had to be taken to the doctor who prescribed a laxative as the antidote to what ailed me.

Ignorance can be, and often was, a source of culinary confusion. Years later, Orlando, an old family friend who had lived in New Jersey for many years, recounted the following story:

"There was a small bodega just down the street from my apartment building in Jersey City. It was there that I shopped for my nightly meals most every night when I wasn't working at the hotel's restaurant as a busboy," he told us in a style worthy of the gifted raconteur he was.

"One could find Cuban bread, frozen foods and canned goods. One of my favorites was canned meat cooked in spices and gravy. I would eat this meat with rice, in sandwich form with Cuban bread and often just by itself. It was delicious.

"After about a year living in the neighborhood the store was sold. The new owner reduced its inventory and I lost my favorite canned meat. I tried other brands as a substitute, but could not find one like it. Eventually, I went up to the new owner and in my broken English inquired about my favorite canned meat. I could not make myself understood and he could not make himself understood. Fortunately, a few days later, a Puerto Rican lady from my building was at the store when I arrived, so I imposed on her to interpret for me," Orlando continued.

"Oh, yes, I know what he's talking about now," said the owner of the bodega. "Tell him that I'm sorry, but we no longer carry canned dog food."

Many similar stories—all true, give a lie or two, I thought—were freely shared among us, the generation transforming into Americans.

At Long Branch apartments, my closest friends were a mix of the newly arrived and those who had lived in the States for a few years. We bonded immediately and together explored Americana. Coca-Cola bottles were passed back and forth on the bleachers by the newly constructed Takoma Park Recreational Center baseball diamond, each time getting colder once the bottle cap had been removed, especially as the cold winter became more intense to prove the theory of the Coca-Cola self-cooling technology we had heard about in Cuba.

Lunch money was collected to purchase Bounty paper towels so that we could see the quicker picker-upper suck water from the ground just like Rosy at the diner in the commercials. It was obvious that we did not have the right technique. And often, we would swear we could see a spark in our teeth after brushing with Ultra-Brite toothpaste.

It was a magical time in our lives. We hungered to prove myths rather than debunk them, but in the end, much as a youth delights in the sleight of hand of a magician while knowing it is just an illusion, we understood these fables were just that. Nonetheless, secretly I hoped I was mistaken. After all, we lived in a land where we knew everything was—and still is—possible.

CHAPTER 15

8702 Gilbert Place

Shortly after the frozen orange concentrate incident, Blanquita took us to our second meeting with the social worker in Silver Spring, Maryland, where it was again explained that the government would help us to establish ourselves by way of providing us with a monthly check, food stamps and free medical assistance. My father grew deeply concerned about this handout that was being offered. He was capable of working. Work was what he needed, not charity.

"It is okay, Pepe," said my mother. "We'll have to get used to the way things are done here, besides, we'll only use it as a loan—you can pay it back later, we'll save our money and pay it back," she reassured him.

Blanca and the four of us visited the welfare office again the following month. We were there to meet our permanent caseworker.

Her name faded from memory many years ago. She was a short, thin woman who had served in the Peace Corps and spoke a little Spanish. Her hair was dark and usually in disarray, her eyes black as the Maryland skies at night. Her face was covered with freckles and her teeth protruded just slightly below her upper lip, parting her mouth just enough to diminish her otherwise natural beauty. She frequently visited our home as she guided us during this important transitional period in our lives.

She ensured that a medical doctor would see us all and that each received a thorough physical. Everyone was given a clean bill of health, except for my grandmother. Abue had a scar in her lung. Tuberculosis, they diagnosed. "Of course, not!" she protested.

The scar had been there for many, many years. Cuban physicians had performed exhaustive testing to determine the actual cause of the scar and found it to be asymptomatic. There was no tuberculosis. Her protests were valid; she had volunteered the issue of the scar on the lung at every medical visit from the time that we had arrived in Miami.

Nonetheless, her protests were of no avail. She was temporarily interned in a hospital near Baltimore about an hour away from our newly acquired apartment at 8702 Gilbert Place in Takoma Park, until a final diagnosis was rendered. As she maintained all along, the scar was asymptomatic and she did not have TB.

Long Branch Apartments was an eclectic mix of immigrants and poor families. It was, however, a great place to start for my family. Many other Cuban immigrants had also settled in this area of Maryland, so we would have other families with whom we shared much in common. I would say that becoming an American really started there for my brother and me.

The brown brick, three-story building with a basement was occupied mostly by Cuban families.

Across from our apartment, at number seven, lived an old Cuban couple with two children. Daisy, their daughter, was in her early thirties. Her features were less than attractive; her charm equaled her lack of beauty. It was 1969, an age and time of change in the midst of a social revolution in America. Daisy, however, saw the world through the eyes of a Cuban peasant who was well into becoming an old maid. Bitterness permeated her being. She was somewhat of a recluse, and never did we hear a kind word from her.

Porfirio, her brother, bordered on that fine line between mental retardation and what we then called normal, he was in his early twenties, tall and heavy, not pleasant to look at, and angry due to years of being taunted and ostracized by his peers.

Only two instances come to mind about Porfirio. The first was during a late October afternoon, just before Halloween of 1969. A small group of those of us in the neighborhood had gathered in front of the building and started a four-on-four game of touch football on the expansive lawn. We took turns at the positions of quarterback and receiver. While I quarterbacked, Porfirio pelted us with his mother's freshly bought eggs with projectile-like precision from the window of his living room. The eggs crashed against my head, just above my forehead. Propelled by the angle, the mostly still remains of the egg deflected off my head and struck Luisito, the smallest and most spirited of our group. Another egg missed its mark. Others splattered on Tony's back and Pili's new jacket.

We immediately ran up the stairs to confront Porfirio. His mother answered the door and rebuked us for accusing her son of such a wicked act. It must have been

71

someone else, she insisted. "Porfirio would never do such a thing." As a good mother, she always defended him. Her protective barrier, however, was pierced almost a year later. My second recollection of Porfirio took place on that day.

Because of my ability to translate developed instinctively and through being my parents' mouthpiece almost from the time that we arrived in the U.S.—not to mention no one else was available—it was requested of my mother that I accompany Porfirio's mother to the Montgomery County Police Station in Silver Spring to interpret for them. Porfirio had been arrested and charged with the crime of having sexually molested a young girl.

As I interpreted, I listened to the charges against him and his responses during the interrogation in his mother's presence.

"Porfirio, tell them you didn't do it," she would cry.

The overwhelming evidence and the testimony of the child left no doubt that Porfirio was guilty of the contemptible act of which he was accused. That was the last time we saw Porfirio.

Another neighbor in our apartment building was *La Marquesa*, as we called her. She was another Cuban exile who had lost her social status upon becoming a refugee, making her not any different from the rest of us. Nonetheless, being of "good breeding," as she repeatedly explained, she still considered herself superior to us in every way. Airs of grandeur accompanied her wherever she went. She had lived in the United States for nearly ten years and resided in the apartment directly below us.

She professed to be well-versed in American social

customs and, more important, what passed for acceptable behavior in American society.

"You cannot walk in boots before seven in the morning during work days," she would say as if reciting the U.S. Code.

"On the weekends, not before nine a.m.," she would add.

Walking on the uncarpeted floor disturbed the sleep of her family and would not be tolerated, she warned.

"There are laws against that type of outrage," she would insist.

Were it to continue, she would have no choice but to call the manager, or worse yet, the police. We listened, and behind her back, Ralph and I mocked her mannerisms and affected speech to amuse ourselves.

Her sons were friendly and good-natured. The youngest played with us regularly and was well-liked. The oldest was a sort of role model. In his mid-twenties, he had attended college and wore a suit to work, unlike the work clothes or uniforms of our parents.

There were many others in the neighborhood that became as close as our own family in our lives. Mrs. Consuegra, "*La alcaldesa*", as all knew her, was willing to espouse and defend any cause on behalf of anyone in our neighborhood. Estrella Taylor was always willing to fry some *frituras* for her sons' friends whenever we visited. Her husband, Rigo, was my father's closest friend. He had found employment at Capitol Drywall & Paint shortly after my father started to work there. It was an eclectic mix of new Americans and repatriates from Appalachia. We lived in relative peace. "*Juntos pero no revueltos*"— meaning together, but not coalesced—my father would often quote the old Cuban axiom.

This, our first home in the United States was a humble place furnished with second-hand furniture and hand-me-downs, but it was a home filled with anticipation of things to come. Most important, it was a home full of love and appreciation for our new life. A used green plaid couch eventually replaced the old one we got from the Adventist Social Services. It was the most valued piece of furniture in the home. It was accompanied by two recently acquired also used solid green fifties style armchairs, two frail and faded side tables, an almost matching coffee table and odd, unmatched lamps. Dark yellow curtains adorned the living room window. It was a large window that looked out over Gilbert Place. The kitchen was compact. It contained a small gas stove, an old refrigerator and worn out linoleum counter.

From the kitchen window we had an unobstructed view of the parking lot behind the apartment building, the Miller Glass company and the Takoma Park Recreation Center—still in its infancy—on Piney Branch Road, and in autumn and winter, when the leaves on the trees would disappear until spring, The Chesapeake Crab House and Bar on University Boulevard to the east, as well as the Esso gas station adjacent to it.

The small dining area contained a newer table and four chairs that had been purchased second hand for a small sum at Toma Furniture on Flower Avenue.

Our bedroom was furnished with two single beds on one side, separated by a few inches the one from the other. A third bed rested against the opposite wall, Abue slept there. My father had strung a cloth line suspended from wall to wall with plant hooks. On it rested a striped blanket. It served as a sort of wall to ensure my grandmother's privacy.

My parent's slept on blankets over a worn mattress on the floor. There was no money to purchase a bed for them, yet. A few weeks later, they bought another old mattress to replace the one from the Adventist Social Services warehouse that they had thrown away without comment. This would be their bed for nearly a year. The transition had started and all was well in Paradise.

CHAPTER 16

Australian Lord of the Seas and A Clown

Our first Christmas came suddenly, or so it seemed. We had been in the United States almost a year, a tremendous milestone. During this time, Ralph and I had gained some proficiency in English. Unabashed, Ralph spoke English freely and was unafraid to make mistakes. I feared being mocked.

Months passed and I still refused to speak English, except in cases of dire need. Perhaps it was a result of a faux pas made by me before moving to our new apartment.

One of the first publications with which I became acquainted was the TV Guide. Channel nine had scheduled what I understood to be a film about pirates, "Captain Kangaroo." Instead, each morning, I found a children's show rather than the able Australian lord of the seas I imagined.

While frantically searching for this movie or adventure series, as I later thought it had to be, since it was scheduled every weekday morning, my curiosity had been piqued by a clown selling hamburgers, his name was *Mezze-Dohnalds*—as best as I could tell—that was the spelling, anyway, M-c-D-o-n-a-l-d-'-s. I wanted to taste a McDonald's hamburger very badly. I asked my aunt about hamburgers and asked where we could find a Mezze-Dohnalds. She said that there was one on Carroll Avenue not too far from our apartment.

My mother finally agreed to take us to the "Golden Arches." Armed with my only phrase: "Excuse me please, me no speak English, only Spanish, where is (fill in the blank)," we embarked on an odyssey to McDonald's. We had walked a mile or so on Carroll Avenue and had been unable to find it.

My pregnant mother was tired and said that if we did not find it soon, we would have to return to the apartment. Alarmed, I sought help from some firemen working outside the Takoma Park Fire Station. My nerves got the better of me and instead of repeating my phrase as usual, "Excuse me please, me no speak English, only Spanish, where is (fill in the blank)," I inverted the key words of the phrase saying, instead, "Excuse me please, me no speak Spanish, only English, where is Mezze-Donalds, please?"

My comical utterance caused the men to erupt with laughter. Not malicious laughter, but rather an innocent reaction to a humorous utterance.

Nonetheless it hurt me deeply. I felt ridiculed and inadequate, useless even for such a small task. I did not wait for their answer. I simply ran away and holding back tears told my mother that it was far away, too far for us to make it in the cold. My confidence had been shattered. I refused to speak English from that day on, unless it was obligated to do so.

CHAPTER 17

Quasar by Motorola

With instamatic Tuner and
Works in a Drawer

As Christmas approached, we would celebrate an American Christmas with gifts and food and all kinds of merriment. A Friday evening, after our ritual of grocery shopping at Giant Foods and the ensuing customary taxi ride back to the apartment—a much looked forward to affair for Ralph and me—we discussed what gifts we would like to have.

Caught in the excitement of the moment I suggested a color television, but not just any TV, the Quasar by Motorola with instamatic tuner and works in a drawer: The Cadillac of all color sets. Ralph agreed. My parents, not expecting such grandiose request from us, simply nodded and eventually celebrated the idea. They came to the Promised Land so that we could enjoy everything American. We would not be denied. The next morning, we walked to Flower Avenue to visit Toma Furniture.

I explained that we wished to purchase a color television. We were shown several models. Already conditioned by Madison Avenue, we opted for the very best in television technology; the aforementioned Quasar by Motorola with works in a drawer. It was a magnificent 25-inch screen closeout model from the previous year. The price was $429.00, but it was worth it, we agreed. It is a good deal, a fair price to pay for such a marvel of American know-how. We would buy it, if we could arrange for a payment plan.

"Credit, you mean?" asked the salesman.

"Yes, credit," I replied as if I knew what it meant.

"Do you have any credit now?" he continued to ask. "I don't understand," I finally admitted.

The television was purchased on lay-away. My parents' bed that they needed would have to wait.

Finally, in the summer of 1970, the much awaited bedroom set, purchased second-hand from a thrift shop in Washington, D.C., just down the street from aunt Blanquita's place on Maple Street, arrived. It was a much celebrated occasion in our home. A real bedroom set, bed included, finally arrived and the bedroom no longer looked as the empty room it had been for over a year.

More and more our American experiences began to shape us, much as a parent teaches a child to take his first steps we were tutored by circumstance and we liked it.

CHAPTER 18

A Question of Style

Summers at the Long Branch apartments were fun-filled experiences of self-discovery. There was also the camaraderie of fellow Cuban immigrants, and the immersion into American culture at school.

Immediately upon moving into our new apartment, we had been accompanied to Rolling Terrace Elementary by our social worker to enroll us in school. I went to Mrs. Moynihan's fifth-grade class, Ralph to Miss Jones' second grade class.

I sat at the back of the classroom and shared my desk with Eddy. He was a rough boy—a minor bully—who was curious by my sudden appearance at his side and my obvious inability to speak English.

Mrs. Moynihan was a wonderful, gifted teacher. She was sensitive and gave special attention to my needs, as well as to those of Susan Wu, an unusually tall girl from China who had also recently started school there. We would stay in her classroom until ten in the morning. At 10, we would go to Mrs. Delgado's ESOL (English for Speakers of Other Languages) class. We, all of us, immediately fell in love with Mrs. Delgado. Not in the physical sense, in the sense of agape, or filial love.

She was in her late forties, or early fifties. She spoke with a thundering raspy voice. Her Spanish was flawless and accentuated with a Cuban flavor. She was American-born, but Cuban raised. We were her children. She loved each one of us with maternal glee. We stayed with her, the Cuban kids of every grade, as well as a small number of other immigrant children, every school day until lunchtime.

Just before the lunch bell, we would each return to our respective classrooms.

When our turn came, each class marched down the halls, past the principal's office and directly to the cafeteria. Five cents would provide us with a complete hot meal and milk. From there we could eat at the tables set up at the all-purpose room or return to our classrooms. Most of us returned to our classroom where we were allowed to play records on the classroom phonograph.

Born to Be Wild, Sunshine of your Smile and other hits of the day would play at moderate modulation while we ate. Russell Iverson usually provided the music. He was a hip kid. Bell-bottomed pants, groovy striped shirt and a neckerchief was his basic wardrobe. I loved the music. I found a safe and happy place in my fifth grade haven.

Kickball and basketball were played daily during the lunch break on the asphalt-covered playground just outside our classroom. I would often ask if I could join in the kickball game. Not being able to detect the slight difference between can and can't, I desisted after attempting to decipher the answer once or twice.

That is how I met my best friend of the next two years, Michael Solomon.

Michael was Jamaican. His father was a professional man—a doctor, I think. He wore shoes with pointed toes and Cuban heels, much as I did. These were a source of laughter to many of our other schoolmates who wore tennis shoes and other less conspicuous footwear.

We made it a point to use Jamaican patois when speaking to one another. It made us even more special.

"Demman't betta dan us, wi ave style," he would often tell me.

"You rite Michael, wi are styling." I assured him. If one would miss school, the other would call and ask: *"Everything criss? Mi neva si yuh a class yestideh."*

We found in each other a source of strength and identity. Much more than with others with whom we shared our culture, such as Gino, a Puerto Rican kid who refused to associate with us, although he spoke Spanish fluently, because he did not wish to be embarrassed by us. Michael and I were rebels. We were happy to be different. We knew we were different, but accepted it and never denied it. Our friendship blossomed at a time of social unrest.

It was a time when blacks that associated with whites were called *Uncle Toms* and Michael was often reminded of this shameful behavior by many of our peers with hands forming a T, much as an athlete would call a time-out. And whites—even those of us who spoke with an accent, and who were "not really white" in their eyes—were called unspeakable names for associating with blacks.

This was our experience during junior high school, when our friendship was eventually torn apart by bigotry and peer pressure on both sides that caused us to become casualties of the racism of the day.

In an eight-grade social studies class moderated by our principal, Mr. Christian, this topic of peer pressure and racial differences was openly discussed. It was one of those rare moments of reflection by adolescent minds. Most of the heads of the different cliques were there in the classroom. Perhaps, this was the reason that the conference took place in our class.

Candid exchanges were voiced. Michael spoke at one point and told of how our friendship had been severed because of the indignity placed upon him by his fellow black students and upon me by my so-called peers. He was not going to be called an Uncle Tom anymore he decided, so he sacrificed our friendship, as did I, in order to be accepted by those who claimed to be our racial equals. It was a moving moment.

At Mr. Christian's suggestion, we crossed the room to shake hands. We embraced and sobbed. Everyone applauded. I had my friend back and the pettiness of racial division ended for us at that point. While racial tensions—albeit minor ones mostly having to do with deciding on whose team one would play—diminished significantly, our friendship never returned to what it had once been, but neither side would ever scrutinize Michael and me again.

"Everything cook an curry, Jorge."

"Everything criss, Michael. Wi are bess friends."

CHAPTER 19

But, We Have Our Bats!

Softball was as foreign to the Cuban students, as the Chinese language would be to a Swiss. "Why did we have to play this girls' game?" we protested. We play baseball!

Baseball! That was what we wanted to play. Anybody could hit a slowly pitched, oversized ball. It did not require much skill. It was beneath us. Catching and throwing a softball was an insult. We played it in P.E., but not by choice. We made sure that all the Cubans were on the same team, and usually played one or two very long innings where our years of sandlot baseball and stick-ball had given us a sharp edge over our American counterparts.

Each time we hit, our opponents would move back, closer to the short fence dividing the asphalt playground from the softball field. They moved back until there was nowhere else to go. Armed with our own baseball bats, unaware softball bats existed or that baseball bats were not allowed in softball, the white orbs would find gaps in the field or go over the fence. Even four of five fielders were useless, as balls would sail over their heads and crash on the hard surface of the basketball courts.

We relished in our athletic superiority. We might lose at kickball and soccer, but softball was our dominion and so it would remain during the summers when we played at the recreation center.

At age thirteen, American Legion Post #41 recruited the entire Cuban clan for Little League Baseball. For the next four seasons we would lose only a handful of games and won championships of some kind almost every year. Physically we were not menacing. Our uniforms were baggy and hot, unlike the ones of most of our competitors. We looked like throwbacks to the teams of the 1920's, while they looked as if Charley Finley himself had selected their wardrobe.

Parents at away games booed us, our ages were challenged often—even though we were smaller and looked younger than most other teams. Our pitchers were accused of throwing illegal pitches when Roberto Consuegra' s breaking balls would move with the effect of an optical illusion.

Juanito Hernandez' fastball could be easily heard, but not clearly seen. And to top it off, we had Marv Stone, who at fourteen could throw hard enough to make every batter not wish to make contact with the ball, even if they could or wanted to, and whose knuckle ball had wicked turns.

These were grand times for the *new* boys of summer in America.

Football, on the other hand, was not a sport that came naturally to us. I first saw a football one late afternoon when coming back from elementary school. I had stayed behind picking crabapples with Ralph, as I now called my brother, and other school kids. As I passed behind the buildings directly across from my own, I saw Robertico Consuegra, Tony Herrera, Richard Herrera (not related) and a few other kids gathering for a game.

"You guys goanna play ball?"

"Yeah," Robertico answered for

me.

"We're going to play football. They want to play."

"Yeah, we want to play," I echoed, running to

change

my clothes and drop the books off at home.

I was on the opposing team to Robertico's. He gave me a brief lesson on the rules of the game and so we started to play. I kicked off by throwing the ball as high and as far as I could. It turned awkwardly and spun horizontally seemingly tumbling and wishing to abandon flight as soon as possible.

"It's a dead duck," Robertico alerted his teammates who quickly ran forward to catch it. I tackled the first person close enough for me to do so, although he did not have the ball.

"You can't do that!" Tony protested. "You can't do that to me, if I don't have the ball!"

Robertico then explained the rule to me pertaining to how one defended the oncoming rush of the returning team. And later, again, he explained about passing from beyond the line of scrimmage, and about pass interference, and about blocking from behind, and about the center having to hike the ball before running with it; and a continuing litany of football rules that still travel in space.

It took a few more games before I was finally chosen, rather than assigned to a side by default. Once I mastered the art of catching the ball, I was more in demand.

By age ten, I was already five-feet and six-inches tall, by twelve a full five-seven and by fourteen, everyone else had passed me and the tallest kid in the group, me, became just an average, if not shorter guy, taller only than my friend Oscar. But for a couple of years, at least, it made me Robertico Consuegra's favorite receiver.

CHAPTER 20

Our Summer of Discovery

Oscar and I were almost inseparable from the time he arrived in Maryland. He lived with his father who was a broadcast engineer. His mother had remained behind in Cuba with his older brother I think I was told.

He arrived at the Long Branch apartments in late April of 1970. We were in Mr. Wright's sixth grade class. We struck an immediate friendship and continued it for many years to come, until our paths diverged and life took us in different directions.

Oscar was short and spoke in a high-pitched voice. His hair was jet-black and his eyes were as blue as the Caribbean waters. This made him a very popular boy with the girls in our circle of friends. He had never lived outside of Miami prior to moving to Maryland. Neither had he seen snow, thus, we spoke at length about it. About sleds and snowball fights, how to build a snowman. And often, as a group, we repeated our adding anatomically correct features to snowmen built by others in the neighborhood. One had been endowed with a very definite masculine feature, while another had been given Mae West like characteristics and a very feminine attribute not needing description.

These tales—true and otherwise—were told over and over to Oscar until he would have skipped summer, if within his powers. His excitement carried over to us too.

As we wandered the streets of Silver Spring between softball and baseball games or frolicking in the newly built swimming pool at the recreation center, we would stop by the hardware store around the block from the Woolworth's to gaze at the latest and most beautiful devise ever invented for winter play: the flying-saucer sled. Fourteen dollars could make one the owner of this silver plated, highly polished wonder of flight in snow. It was beautiful.

Every one of us had lusted most of the summer after this radiant temptress clumsily displayed among tools, transistor radios and other products forgotten in the display window. Tony, Oscar, Mike, and I decided to pool resources and save our money for the purchase of the sled.

Our parents had failed to see the usefulness of such a practical winter wonder—especially this far removed from the snow season. In a matter of weeks—months, actually—just before school started, we had accumulated the handsome sum of six dollars. Assured in the knowledge that we could raise the money before snowfall, we used the funds, instead, to purchase a cheap basketball. It was a logical move at the time, or so it seemed, since we played basketball every day on the asphalt half court by Sligo Creek, just beyond our apartments by the school-bus stop.

It was a glorious summer. While our parents were at work, we played with relentless joy and an adventuresome spirit. We sailed makeshift vessels on the currents of the shallow Sligo creek. Wars had been won and lost by combinations of armies defending their territory. At some point, each one of us had been captured and made to suffer the only form of torture allowed: tickling or being struck on the shoulders. Our circle had bonded these very different Cuban boys. Our strength came from our loyalty to each other. There were no secrets between us. It was a summer of discovery and of defining our own identities.

American Legion Post #41 continued its baseball terror on our more elegant, athletic and handsome opponents. Countless hours were spent on the field on the hill above the recreation center shagging fly balls, taking batting practice and playing occasional pick-up games with our fathers.

Willie Miranda lived in Baltimore and frequently stopped to play with his fellow Cuban expatriates. He was a former big leaguer who at one time played with the Washington Senators. Tony Taylor of the Philadelphia Phillies was Tony Herrera's uncle and also frequented our humble neighborhood while visiting his sister Estrella. Other older boys were scouted and at times sought after by colleges and professional teams.

Baseball was a way out for many of us. Most important, it was our game. We delighted in its simplicity and beauty. Our mastery of this sport so loved by the Cuban people was a common bond that held the generations together and strengthened our associations.

It was on this field that we also discovered other of life's great offerings. Our first girlfriends, our first romantic kiss, holding hands tenderly and playing roles reserved for this rite of passage from boyhood to manhood. We had seen our very first Playboy centerfold on this field. Some reacted differently than others. I felt I had aided and abetted to the commission of some great crime, so I hyperventilated and vomited at the mere thought of being punished for such a wicked act.

The new pool was also a place of discovery for us. We swam in its cool waters to refresh our bodies from the heat and humidity of the hot Maryland summer. We played whatever games they were willing to dish up at the recreation center, and also developed a friendship with Fernando who attended the University of Maryland and worked the *rec* part-time to earn pocket money. He taught us that education, not baseball, was the way out and became influential in molding our view of how to achieve the American Dream.

All in all, I can't think of a happier time in my life. A time when the world was for the taking and the spirit of youth lived to its fullest in each of us.

CHAPTER 21

Blue Team, White Team
And Voices from the Lockers

September found us in school again. My friends and I had started at Takoma Park Junior High School. This was a tremendous change in our lives. We were growing up.

On the first day of school we looked for our names on the bulletin board outside the cafeteria hallway. It listed our classes, teachers, classroom numbers and our being assigned to the white or blue team. Only Tony Herrera and me were on the blue team, the other boys were on the white team. There wasn't much explanation pertaining to these teams, other than this week was blue and the next white.

We did not truly understand what the significance of being assigned to either the white or blue team was. We assumed that things would fall into place eventually, as surely someone would guide us into our new routine beyond elementary school. I followed my class schedule and reported to the gym on the first day; it concluded without any major disruption or embarrassment.

Tuesday, I followed my class assignment as the day

before. All went well until it came time for gym class. I reported to the gym, and entered the locker room. All the faces were different. Mr. MacArthur, the basketball coach, said to me in his usual playful style, "Hey, rookie, didn't I see you here yesterday. Today is white team, kid, go on to your other class."

"Other class?" I asked myself. "What other class?" I left the gym and sneaked past the classrooms down the long corridors hoping to avoid teachers and find one of my friends. As I moved from one end of the school to the next, I found Tony Herrera hiding in the bathroom. He was as confused as I was. We tried to make sense of our situation, but could not. That being the case, we stayed in the bathroom standing on toilet seats in adjacent stalls until the next bell. From there the day fell into place again.

On the school bus ride back home, we asked Richard and Oscar about this unusual class situation. Richard had gone to art class on Monday and Tuesday was his gym day. Oscar had hidden in the storage area outside the gym after not hearing his name in roll call at the beginning of gym class. He was on the white team, but he too was out of place.

On Wednesday, all three of us did the most logical thing that we could come up with. We hid ourselves in the old, cavernous, empty lockers on the hallway leading to the auditorium and band room. Our cover did not last long. The voices rattling off in Spanish from inside the lockers attracted the attention of a passerby, Mr. Anderson, our science teacher, who yelled at us and educated us on the sin of skipping class.

"Where are you guys supposed to be?" he asked.

Our shrugged shoulders revealed our ignorance while freeing us from the crime of which we had been accused.

"Let me see your schedules?" He said. "Okay, you go to Mrs. Adler's art class," he pointed to me. "You go with him," he told Tony, and you go to Mr. Kalandro's shop class," he instructed Oscar.

Our dilemma having been resolved we went on our way and reported to our respective classes. Aside from the brief and casual interrogatory by Mrs. Adler, "are you boys in this class?" there were no other ill effects upon any of us.

Eventually everything made sense. On blue week, we had gym on Monday, Wednesday and Friday. Tuesday was wood shop with Mr. Huff and Thursday art class with Mrs. Adler. On white week, Monday we had shop with Mr. Huff; Wednesday art with Mrs. Adler and Friday, shop with Mr. Kalandros again; gym on Tuesday and Thursday. The art and shop classes alternated schedule every third week.

Junior high school also offered new dietary choices to us. Candy bars were sold freely at hallway stands to raise funds for a variety of clubs; to us it was breakfast. Lunch also offered a variety of diverse selections and there were Coke machines in the cafeteria. Life was good.

Lunch recess was the highlight of our day. We would share a table and discuss the day's events, girls, jokes to be played, the proper technique for throwing a curve ball, and activities for after school. Jokes of incredibly poor taste were perpetrated on fellow classmates during lunch, and the daily ritual of the basketball game never failed us.

Jungle ball, a game where rules were suggested, but not followed, and short of blood, no foul was called. It was played at its best on the outdoor basketball courts of Takoma Park Junior High School. Oscar Robertson, Earl The Pearl Monroe, Lew Alcindor, Elgin Baylor, Walt Frazier and many others were poorly imitated.

"Did you see my fade-away shot?" Oscar would ask.

"That's a Big-O move," he would say referring to his rendition of the Oscar Robertson patented shot.

"That's nothing!" Richard would say, "Dig this Chamberlain hook," while his wide body mimicked the seven-foot center of the Los Angeles Lakers. "Swoosh," he would add, "nothing, but net."

Even the coldest day would find us shooting hoops in the many half-courts of schools and playgrounds nearby. Our frolics of youth continued well into the Thanksgiving break. In between, we had attended parties, deciphered school schedules and taken pleasure in the carefree condition of our youth.

CHAPTER 22

Oscar and the Magic Sled

It was just after Thanksgiving when the Maryland skies exploded into a breathtaking spectacle. A veritable myriad of tiny sculptures fell on our tongues, hands and hair as we looked at the canopy of heaven. The snow accumulated on the glistening streets of Long Branch apartments. By morning, we awoke to nearly ten inches of snow. I quickly clothed myself and ate the hot breakfast that my mother had prepared for us. Ralph was just as anxious.

The sounds of WFAN, our Spanish-language radio station where I would work in a few years and start my career in broadcast journalism, became as sweet as the sound of angelical harps and cherubim voices.

"The following school districts have cancelled classes for today: Anne Arundel County schools, Howard County schools, Prince Georges County Schools and Montgomery County Schools in Maryland. Arlington County schools will start classes an hour later."

Providence had intervened. A miracle had occurred. God really did love me. He loved us all, I thought. With His divine intervention, it was assured that my mother would not hinder our day in the snow.

"George!" a voice shouted from below. "Hey, George!" he continued.

Standing in the lightly falling snow stood Oscar. His diminutive presence aroused with the possibilities of the day.

"Hey, George," he yelled, as I parted the living room window curtain just enough to be able to communicate, while avoiding my mother's ire.

"There's no school, today. Tell your mom ... tell her you need to come out to play in the snow."

This was Oscar's first-ever experience with snow. This was the culmination of one of his life's dreams. His pleas to a higher being had being answered as we witnessed an incredible feat of good fortune—a miracle of sorts— given that snow rarely fell prior to December in Maryland. It had been a tremendous, delightful surprise for us all.

"Mom, can we play in the snow?" I eagerly asked.

"I don't know," she replied. "It's awfully cold out there and I don't want you boys getting sick."

She worried too much about us getting sick. That was her disease. She suffered from a malady that caused her to think that every act, outside of going to school or church, could be the culprit of some incredible illness, an open invitation for the grim reaper himself to take us to his dark dominion.

"I'll wear my gloves and my hat..." I pleaded.

"Me too." added Ralph.

Oscar had come up the three flights of stairs and stood by the now partially open door at the doorway, his shivering body covered by a dark brown overcoat two sizes too small. It was the same one he had worn since the start of school.

His head was covered with a long-sock knit cap that could well have served him as a scarf. A real spectacle of winter preparedness—save for his feet. He still wore low-cut shoes with two-inch heels and pointed toes. While they were finely polished and elegant in any other occasion, being worn on a cold, snowy morning accentuated his caricature-like appearance.

This snowy Maryland day would be the setting for an odyssey of youth never to be forgotten and oft remembered. It was the day that has come to be known as the day of Oscar and the magic sled.

At first, we simply admired the falling snow. It was light and the skies filled with finely detailed miniature sculptures. Oscar would playfully catch some on his tongue, and marveled at each crepuscule that would land on his brown coat. I had often looked at snow in the same way—examining each flake—amazed by the detailed weave and design.

The ground was soft and it appeared that we walked on clouds. It was nothing like Oscar had imagined. It was not wet. It was not slippery. It was not many things that he thought it would be. But, it was wonderful. Wonderful beyond any expectation his heart and mind could have conjectured.

We slowly walked toward Rolling Terrace Elementary, just a few blocks down the road. It seemed the ideal place to start our day. On snowy days, the rolling hill that the school stood upon served as an excellent winter playground. All we needed was a sled.

As we reached the school, we could see many of our classmates and their siblings fly through the air in their wondrous snow contraptions. We stood on the sidewalk at the foot of the small hill awestruck by the spectacle.

I recalled having seen a discarded sled on the bed of Sligo Creek. It was twisted and rusted, but the adage about beggars not being choosy crept to the forefront of my mind. Pride has its limitations, after all, especially in the blithe boldness of youth. My idea was well received.

We quickly headed to search for the Holy Grail of twisted steel and rotted wood. It was still there, but it was in much worse shape than I recalled. There was little hope of recapturing its usefulness, much less the splendor of its youth.

"Hey, guys," Ralph, said. "I know where we can find a big sled," he reluctantly offered.

"Yeah, right..." Oscar protested. "You don't know nothing ... *comebasura.*"

"Hey, don't call him names," I immediately replied launching the customary, and very much obligatory, punch to the shoulder, a way of asserting our manhood and protecting the honor of a loved one without offending the recipient of the physical reprisal.

"I'm telling the truth," Ralph insisted. "I know where we can find a big "Flying Whammo sled."

"Where?" I asked. "And you better not be lying to us," I warned my portly younger brother.

"By the Adventist house," he retorted.

The Adventist house was a place well known to Ralph and me. In the summer, we often found our way there while playing war. It was a one floor building with large glass windows. It stood just on the other side of a fence that did not quite reach the ground, leaving a gap of about two feet between its lowest row of chain link and the loam it was supposed to reach. On the other side of the fence there was a swimming pool. It was rarely, if ever, used. The Adventist house, as we called it, was a retirement home, much like the one where my mother cooked.

Having a pool there never made sense to us. So, maybe they had a sled there too. Or maybe it was abandoned outside the welfare thrift shop ran by the Adventist church next to the old folks home from whence we acquired many a household item for our apartment.

"Okay," I said. "We'll go take a look ... "

As we started on our way there, we retraced our steps, then realized it would be much faster if we walked back to the school, continued past the apartments at the end of Barron Street and climbed the hill to its left that lead to the Adventist house. As we reached the street, we heard our names being called, "Hey, Jorge ... wait!" It was Tony and his cousins Pedro and Eusebio whom were better known as Pili and Chachao respectively. These were our best friends, our partners in crime, so to speak. And on this one day, not far from being an actual crime.

"What are you guys, doing?" Tony asked.

"We're goanna' get a sled," Oscar quickly replied.

"Can we come with you guys?" asked Chachao.

"Sure. Let's go. We'll have a groovy time," said Oscar.

Tony and his cousins were never far from us. We lived just a couple of buildings away from each other, but most of our time was spent together at school, in the baseball diamonds and at decrepit basketball courts in our neighborhood. There was never any rivalry between us. Even as we grew into our rebellious teenage years, we remained the best of friends. No one ever came between us, and while others would attempt to thwart our friendship along racial divides, it prevailed true. And so it lasted well into early adulthood, until Oscar, Tony, Pili and Chachao moved to Miami and followed the sudden migration south that took place in the mid-seventies.

But this day was a day when the mischief brought about by innocence and misguided desires would rule. Together the six of us climbed the slippery hill that overlooked the nursing home.

"Where is it?" Oscar asked as we looked at the white-covered cement below us.

"There ... "Ralph whispered.

"Where?" I asked emphatically of my younger brother.

"Under the umbrella," he answered.

Ralph pointed to the round metallic tabletop from which an umbrella passed through a hole in its center.

Its white enamel base covered in snow. It was not difficult to see, even at first sight, that it could make a functional sled. A "Flying Whammo" of sorts that could serve as the alpine instrument of joy, we so desired.

"Are we going to steal it?" asked Tony.

"I'm not stealing anything," I said, fearful of what my mother would do to me, should I engage in one of the most shameful sins known to mankind.

"Well, maybe we don't steal it...we just borrow it," said Oscar.

We looked at each other to see if anyone would object to Oscar's brilliant conclusion.

"You mean we'll bring it back?" I asked.

"Sure. We just use it on the other side of the hill, just behind us, so we don't have to even go far with it," he explained.

"But, how are we going to take it without getting in trouble?" Pili wondered.

"We just take it. Nobody's going swimming today, anyway," said Oscar.

"I don't know." I said aloud, concerned with the potential outcome of being caught with the table in our possession. I was always a cautious person. Stealing was not something that I took lightly.

As I recall that day, I can still picture all of us, each a little more than a child sharing a bond of friendship as we would never know again.

I can also still see each one of us in my mind's eye filled with the anticipation of play and the resolve to commit a petty crime while justifying our deeds.

"Well, are we going to do it or not?" Oscar demanded.

"Come on *plastic*," laughed Tony calling me by the nickname he had given me for reasons still unclear to this day.

"Or are you too chicken? Quack, quack, quack," he cackled.

"That's a duck, you idiot," Oscar protested. My temper would flare up with any dare—well, almost any and he knew it. This would be an acceptable one.

The snow continued to fall, even as we discussed the prospect of borrowing the tabletop that would serve as our sled.

"Come on guys!" Oscar said in frustration. "I'm freezing my butt off."

Oscar's nose was flushed red and his body shook ever so slightly, his muscles shivering attempting to create some warmth.

"All right!" I said. "Oscar, Tony, let's go. We'll take the table. Pili, Chachao and Ralph, you guys keep your eyes open."

Cautiously, the three of us started our descent toward the gaping hole on the fence that separated us from the soon-to-be sled. We hid in the cover of the trees that abounded on the hill and slid the final few feet toward the fence.

Quietly, we crept under it, through the gaping slit that served as a portal to the pool area. Tony took his lookout position on our side of the fence keeping his eyes on the large, rectangular, panoramic window of the nursing home's recreation room.

"It's okay...all clear "he whispered. "Go ahead ..."

Oscar and I continued poolside on the other side of the barrier and engaged in our task of removing the umbrella and the tabletop from the tripod legs that supported them with the skill and deliberate tranquility of Alexander Monday, one of our favorite TV characters.

In my mind, this was not the theft of a metal table anymore, it was the heist of a fine work of art in one of Europe's greatest museums whose name I could not pronounce, or a valuable jewel cache from the Tower of London itself.

In just a few minutes we were able to free the table from its base and started the trek back to the top of the hill.

Tony pulled on the chain-link fence with an upward motion to facilitate our getaway.

Oscar and I nervously carried the heavy tabletop inches off the ground in a crouched position carefully avoiding contact with the snow-covered cement and attempting to maintain the required stealth and sure footing as we walked. Oscar battled his shoes intent on betraying him.

Finally, we cleared the fence and found ourselves at the foot of the hill. I, being the tallest, started to pull on the table by securing a sure grip with my fingers around the lip of the tabletop. Oscar pushed from below at the other end on an incline.

The uphill climb was difficult. The snow had turned to slippery powder. I struggled to keep traction, often falling in a sitting position uphill to maintain control and retain a grip on the item.

There was a quiet reverence about us as we perpetrated our great theft. It was, perhaps, this somberness—the solemnity of the moment—that caused Ralph to break the silence.

"Hey, guys ...", he whispered, "here comes the nurse ... she's coming this way..." he said raising his voice while running away.

This was a most inappropriate moment for a nine-year-old to pull his first prank. We panicked. I gasped, petrified with fear, and in the stupor of the moment loosened my grip and allowed the tabletop to leave my hands. I only realized this as I heard a loud thump and a thud, as Oscar, with the table now on top of him, was overpowered by the metallic circle causing him to slide on his back to the original point of entry on our side of the hill. Just barely visible was his head protruding from under the table that now held him down in the snow.

I looked at him with pity, the terror in his eyes tantamount to a silent scream. Tony continued to look at the building intently seeking to find the nurse Ralph had announced. She was nowhere in sight.

Oscar, panicked by his abrupt descent, pushed the table off, then shrieked and let out an obscene litany riddled with every curse word ever created, as well as a few new ones that he aptly improvised for the occasion.

He attempted to run uphill, but his lack of traction because of his shoes caused him to fall on his back repeatedly in a downward spiral.

"Come on, Oscar, hurry up!" we shouted.

A small group of nurses now looked through the big window.

Oscar kept falling in projectile-like manner, until finally, he came to a stop with a thundering crash against the chain-link fence. The discarded table, now leaning against the fence, danced from side to side against metal noisily sounding an alarm for our capture.

"Come on, man, they're going to call the *Fuzz* ..." someone said.

Oscar desperately attempted to climb the slick ramp he had created on the way down. It was a comedic tragedy of cinematic proportions.

"Help me!" he cried as he struggled to make his way back to us.

We were frightened, but the sight of Oscar's plight was mesmerizing. We could not look away. We were spellbound by the spectacle. His feet advancing just a few inches before, as if by magnetic pull, crashing backwards on the slick slope, made more slippery with each attempt to escape. Suddenly, we erupted overcome with laughter, save Oscar who swore an epithet seldom heard since.

As one of the nurses opened the recreation room door to gain a better view of the situation, one I'm sure she did not completely comprehend. Oscar miraculously devised his escape. He took off his pointy toed Cuban heel shoes and ran, leaving perfectly formed tiny footprints in the snow, all the way to the top of the hill.

As his safe return was assured, we all took off running from the scene of the crime, followed by Oscar and his obscene tirade in tow.

CHAPTER 23

"As Far as the Airwaves Take Us"

Throughout most of my life there has been a constant at my side, even if not in the literal sense—Fermín. My father chose Fermín to stand as godfather at my baptism in the Catholic Church. Family tradition dictated every child be baptized. It was an inescapable rite. Being a godfather or a godmother—religion aside—was a duty not taken lightly.

Abuela Cari was my godmother. Perhaps, because Fermín assumed this duty or simply because he is my mother's older brother, he became a second father to me and one of my closest friends. He passed away in 2016. I was his confidant. He was someone I trusted and loved, and I knew he loved me.

Known for my temper tantrums from an early age, my mother found different ways to curtail my mischief. On one occasion where I had become exceedingly unruly, she thought that suitable punishment on that day would be to lock me in Fermín's electrical repair shop atop the roof of our house in Guanabacoa. It was a small concrete room with a workbench where he would solder resistors, capacitors, inductors, and replace tubes to resurrect old radios or other electrical gadgets. Unfortunately, the outcome was not what my mother hoped for, but a logical one to a raging four-year-old. Within a few minutes and before my mother could open the door and turn on the lights to stop the destruction, I had shattered, smashed or otherwise made irreparable a substantial portion of his inventory. My parents were shocked by the havoc I had created and puzzled as to how they would explain it to my uncle. Fermín just said, "Don't hit or punish him, I would have done the same thing if stuck in a dark room," and walked away unfazed.

In another country and another time, during the same snow storm that found Oscar, Ralph, Tony, Pili, Chachao and me mesmerized by the snowfall of that November day, Fermín decided he too wanted to enjoy the wintery carnival atmosphere that permeated our neighborhood.

"I had bought these for Christmas. Merry Christmas!" Fermin said as he handed me a small box with two walkie- talkies from Radio Shack.

"Wow! These are great!" I said. "Thanks, Fermi," as I called him.

"I thought I would take one and start walking and see how far we can use them."

"Perfect," I said.

"Go up to the apartment so we can extend the range," he instructed.

I ran the six flights of stairs and watched through the window as he headed down Barron Street paralleling Sligo Creek.

"Are you cold," I asked.

"Nah," he replied, "had a little shot of Bacardi before I left the house."

We communicated using our radios for around ten minutes. After that, only a faint voice crackling on the frequency could be heard. I stood my post faithfully for over an hour, watching television and periodically attempting to make contact.

Eventually, my mother insisted that I go to bed in spite of my protests about abandoning my communication post. I turned the walkie-talkie off and went to bed. Then, almost immediately, I turned the two-way device on again, turned the volume almost all the way down, and hid under the covers in case Fermín called.

My cousin Lily laughed at her father's adventure from the previous night.

"He's like a little kid. Can you believe he walked all the way down to Flower Avenue and then to Piney Branch and to the D.C. line?" Lily told her friend, Katy Amaro, as we walked to school.

"A kid? No, an adult that knows how to have fun," I declared, avowing to be just like my uncle when I grew up.

That brief moment of discovery of using the airwaves was followed by lengthy discussions about radio frequencies on different broadcast bands. Such was Fermín's influence on me that that small incident led me to pursue and receive my amateur radio license years later to share something we both loved doing together. He loved to learn and understand technologies. He instilled that love of learning in me, as well as one to better myself and to never enjoy the little things in life. I'm forever grateful for his having been in my life for reasons too numerous to count.

CHAPTER 24

Textiles, Betrayal and "The Visit"

By 1971 we had become more acclimated to our almost American life. Our circle of friends had been expanded for my parents as well as for my brother and me. Other close relatives had reached U.S. soil that year. My two closest friends, confidents and caretakers, beside my parents, were my identical twin cousins Azalea Amelia and Amelia Azalea. Their father had, if anything, been creative when naming them.

Identical in every way, except for their very distinct and strong personalities, they had settled in Harrison, New Jersey with their mother, Carmen and their dad, Mario. Carmen was more of a sister than an aunt to my mom as they were approximately the same age and had been raised together by my great-grandmother.

We visited them frequently, as they did us. It was during one of our weekend stays at their home that a life-changing event took place and an old umbrage redressed.

The first event was an unexpected visit from one of my dad's former business associates whom my father had not seen in over ten years and of whom he was unaware of being in the U.S. He had married the daughter of my father's uncle and mentor who started him in the textile industry. They had recently relocated to Union City, New Jersey after having lived in North Carolina for several years.

Union City was home to a thriving, large Cuban-American community. The reunion took place when the daughter of my dad's relative attended the wedding of one of my cousins' friends. As they talked they discovered the family connection to my father. She was told that we lived in Maryland and of our frequent visits to the Garden State.

The impromptu reunion was particularly pleasing to my father. Aside from my mother, my brother and me, he had no other relatives in the States. This created a sense of him not being so alone and detached from other relatives, even distant ones.

Later that evening, dad asked my mom, my brother and me to sit around my cousins' kitchen table to discuss a job offer his relative made him earlier in the day. He was offered a position as Chief Mechanic at a textile factory in Elizabeth, New Jersey. The pay would be more than triple what he was earning as a house painter in Maryland.

"We'll be able to buy a house," he said. "In a good neighborhood with good schools," he added timidly, uncertain of how we would react, although it was obvious that our misgivings showed in our faces.

To us, New Jersey and New York were not places where one would want to live. Driving through Newark on our first visit, we had been stopped at a police road-block and detoured as two people had been shot and laid dead in the street. This disturbed us to the point of considering immediate return to the relative safety of

Silver Spring, Maryland.

On our second visit, about a month later, on a Saturday afternoon while driving to a record shop to buy Cuban music, two men brutally fought over double-parking with knives drawn. Subsequent to those incidents, I often chose to stay home with my grandmother rather than travel to New York, as we did not really understand that Harrison, New Jersey and Manhattan were two different cities in two different states.

I panicked at the possibility of having to live in a place I feared so much. My brother's terrified look also spoke volumes. My mother listened with her head lowered, but did not respond. It was obvious to my father that we would follow him, but reluctantly. Being the man he was, he did not pursue it further and quickly alleviated our fears.

"You know; I think I'm going to turn him down. We came here to be happy. Money does not mean happiness. I don't mind being a painter. If you're happy, then, we stay where we are. Besides, I think things are much too expensive here anyway. But I wanted to let you know about the offer, that was all."

The matter was never brought up again. There were no *what if 's* or *should haves* ever raised by dad. I did not truly understand his great sacrifice until it was much too late to make amends.

Something that happened that same weekend was dramatic and allowed me to see another side of my father I had never seen before. José Mena did not believe in revenge, but he did believe in honesty, fair dealing and righting wrongs. Some things needed to be resolved, "as a matter of principle," he explained.

Eduardo was a friend of many years in Cuba. His son and two daughters frequently played at our house, as our fathers visited or worked on projects in our respective homes.

For a period of several weeks during the summer of 1968 our days had been spent at Cojimar on the beach.

Cojimar was where my maternal great-grandfather Francisco Hernández, whom we called Abuelo, lived well into his nineties before being relocated by the government to a shared cottage. Later he died at the incredible age of 102 or 106, depending on whom you asked.

The beach was about half an hour by bus from Calle Apodaca in Guanabacoa and it was a second home to us. My father kept a boat there. He had built it with Fermín and Fermín's Cuban-Chinese brother-in-law Evelio Chang. The vessel was appropriately christened, The *Tres Amigos*.

Dad would row the boat for hours around Cojimar with my brother and Eduardo's children on board. Other times, our mothers would join us. And it was not unusual to see both our families in the small fishing vessel navigate from the lighthouse to the coves on the north shore and on to the eastern shallow waters across from my great-grandfather's large beach home. We mostly rowed, but its homemade mainsail would be raised from time to time allowing the harnessed wind to push the heavy boat through the blue-green waters.

As summer turned to autumn, we often found ourselves fishing late into darkness in search of one more fish to add to our day's catch. Our excursions were so frequent and eventually so commonplace that the local militiamen and coastguard became well acquainted with my father, Eduardo and each of us children.

In our minds, the objective was clearly explained: the more fish we have, the better we eat. However, as with all else in Cuba under communism, things often were not what they seemed.

One evening in September of 1968, my mother asked us to go to bed shortly after dinner. She told us we would go see Abuelo who was not feeling well later that evening. Eduardo would drive us, it was explained, as he often did in his ancient American sedan.

Later that night, dad woke us up and mom helped us get dressed. I noticed we were all dressed in black. I surmised that, perhaps, Abuelo was dying and that we were preparing ourselves to mourn him. Tears nearly trickled down my cheeks.

"Is Abuelo dead, mom?" I asked.

"What? No. Why would you ask that?" she

replied. "We're dressed in black."

She smiled. "No, Papo, it's just what we're wearing tonight. That's all."

I was not convinced, but it was evident the topic was not to be continued, as the unspoken rule was: If they are lying to you and they know you know it, leave it alone.

The vigil lasted well past midnight, at which point Ralph had been asleep for hours on a chair and I had dozed off repeatedly on the couch. My father was frustrated, fearful and angry. His words to my mom evolved from concern, to fear and ultimately to realizing that he had been betrayed. That night, both our families,

Eduardo's and ours, were supposed to leave Cuba on my father's boat.

Had all gone as planned, we would have rowed past the breakers that night. Eventually my dad would have raised the sail sewn out of empty flour bags by my father on an industrial machine with their blue logo distended as the wind would push the large fishing boat. It was the type of boat commonly used by Cojimar's fishermen to catch Marlin, Swordfish and other smaller aquatic life into deep waters. It was a vessel similar to the one used by the Old Man in Hemingway's *The Old Man and the Sea*.

It was three years later now, and through my dad's relative, Armando Arce, my father found the whereabouts of Eduardo. Since our relative was unaware of what had transpired on that October night, he thought Eduardo, now a successful textile mechanic himself, would be surprised and happy to see his old coworker and friend: my father.

Muscular and strong, my father could be an imposing figure. Having been a former boxer, he carried himself with a certain confidence derived from mastering the skill of unarmed combat. His quiet demeanor somehow made him seem even more formidable when raised to anger; rare for him. My Uncle Fermín, my Uncle Mario—the twins' father—my dad and me drove to an underground parking about a block from the brownstone where Eduardo lived with his family in Queens, New York. We waited for over an hour before he arrived.

He drove a late model, Buick Elektra. As he drove to a parking lot on the corner a few yards from his house, he squinted through the windshield in disbelief at seeing my father standing across the street from his home.

A few minutes later he approached the house and any doubt of the person outside his home actually being my father vanished.

"Pepe?" Eduardo asked his eyes projecting a mix of bewilderment and dread.

My father quietly crossed the street with my uncles and me following close behind.

"Yes, Pepe." my father replied with no emotion in his voice.

"Can we go inside?" my father asked.

"Yes. Of course." Eduardo said.

Eduardo, a large man, was pale and moved cautiously as if expecting my father to pounce on him at any moment. It was that quiet, controlled deportment that made my father seem even more ominous. Unpredictability, I found, can be a powerful weapon. It certainly was that day.

We entered the brick brownstone in Queens. Eduardo's wife, who came to the door to greet her husband, halted her approach in shock and walked backwards unable to speak.

"Is there a place we can talk in private?" my father asked.

The two men went into a study off the living room and closed the door behind them. There was no violence. Voices were not raised. The wife simply stood by the door nervously cleaning her hands on a large apron.

"And your mother?" she asked, breaking the heavy silence.

"She's fine." I nervously replied. "How is Eduardito?" I asked of my former friend.

"He goes to a military school," she answered half smiling.

We simply stood there for what seemed to be hours, but I suppose were only just a few minutes. The puzzling image of my father coming out of the room with his old portable shortwave radio in hand—the same one Eduardo had brought on the sea voyage from Cuba—was unexpected at best and bizarre to say the least.

"We can go now," he said having settled his affairs in some odd way.

Quietly, Fermín, Mario and I headed for the door. My father approached Eduardo's wife who seemed to be frozen by fear and gently took her by the hands, the radio under his arm.

"This has nothing to do with you," dad told her. She pulled her hands away opened her arms and hugged my father crying and repeating, "I'm sorry…I'm so sorry." My father embraced her and gave her a kiss on the forehead.

That was the last time we talked to or saw Eduardo or his family. Neither of my uncles asked what had taken place. My father seemed satisfied. We simply drove back to Harrison, New Jersey.

A few days later, back home, I overhead my father tell my mother that Eduardo suspected my father was armed and would kill him. He said Eduardo pleaded for his life and that of his family. My father was taken aback by Eduardo's reaction given that dad was not a violent man by nature. Instead my father responded with the only words he could think of.

"Do you have my radio?" which caused Eduardo to become inexplicably even more frightened.

"I'll give you money. I have some cash in my desk."

Eduardo opened a drawer and pulled out an envelope with twenty and fifty dollar bills. He handed it to my father who, bewildered and offended—as he told my mother—threw it back at him.

"I just wanted you to know that cowards and traitors have no place to hide," my father told him.

"No money can repay your disloyalty, Eduardo. Enjoy your new life, and remember you have it because you betrayed a friend and a brother."

As I overheard my father's account, I was proud of him, if not somewhat disappointed for his not having meted some physical punishment on the man that I now knew had so deeply hurt him.

CHAPTER 25

Take a Right at Atlantic Avenue

In spite of our bad experience with Eduardo, the beach continued to be a part of our identity and culture. We grew on the sands of Cuba's beaches and learned to swim in its Caribbean-bathed shores. It was only logical we would continue our beach-faring ways in our new land.

Virginia is for lovers. That's what my t-shirt said, and the bumper sticker on Julián's car and the tote bag where my mother carried our sunscreen, sandwiches, towels and everything else we needed to establish our spot on the sands off the boardwalk in Virginia Beach.

This had become our summer getaway. My parents, Cora and Julian with their four children—Tony, Albert, Marisol and Willy—Fermín with his wife Ana, whom we called Tana, and my two my cousins, Liliana and Aurora, vacationed there at least a week during the summer and almost every three-day weekend between the end of school and just prior to school starting again.

We stayed at the Bulwark Motel. It was not on the

main drag on Atlantic Avenue, but it was economical and—apparently—any rule as to how many guests could stay in a room was not enforced. This also applied to the many hotplates plugged in nightly for the evening meal, often times consisting of the catch of the day. When our blankets brought from home were insufficient to create comfortable sleeping arrangement for the kids, Fermín would help himself to the long pool chairs at night and bring them to our packed rooms as additional beds.

The couple that ran the place was aware of our shenanigans, but never said a word since I suspect we were some of their best customers. Eventually, our group decided that we needed one big room for everybody—an apartment with a kitchenette—to meet our needs. So, my mom and me scouted around and found an equally low- budget setup at a reasonable price with a couch that turned into a sleeper, black and white nine-inch TV, old dinette table, and a small kitchen with a fridge. We could say goodbye to the coolers, and we did.

During one of our visits to a grocery store, I saw the butcher packing chicken necks in a bucket of ice.

"What are the chicken necks for?" I asked.

"For crabbing," said the older black man with a heavy southern accent.

"Do you use hooks?" I asked genuinely interested in the answer.

"Oh, no, son—you tie a string, toss 'em and wait a while," he carefully explained.

"Then, you wait for the crab to get a hold of 'em and

start eating the chicken. They be holding on so strong to the neck, they think the pull on the string is the tide, but you got to do it nice and gentle-like—they just keep on eating'."

"Does it really work? Can you catch enough crabs to cook for dinner?"

"Yes sir," he laughed, "with the chicken necks and the feet. Don't make them no difference no how. They just want to eat. And if you pull them strings all gentle and soft like I said, you'd be having a big pot of steamed Chesapeake Blue Crab tonight," he assured me emphasizing his last phrase.

"But won't the waves make it hard for them to see the chicken?" I inquired.

"Oh, my," he said feigning surprise. "You've really never done this before have you?"

"No, sir. I've never fished crabs before."

"Crabbing'," he corrected. "Not fishing. Crabbing." He paused and looked at me.

"Now you talk a little different than we do down here, so I'm a-going to say you Italian or—"

"Cuban. Sir." My family is from Cuba."

Well, that don't no matternone, long as you not one of the New Yorkers coming here to mess with our town folk. Look here young fellow, do you have a car?"

"Yes sir. My momma drives a 1962 Ford Fairlane 500," I explained in detail, as it seemed that the year, make and model were necessary when replying about anything having to do with our vehicle.

"Good. That'll get you there…the place I'm going to show. I swear you'll catch more crab than you can eat—but wait—Who's going to cook 'me?" my new friend asked.

"My father is a cook and so is my momma…and my uncles. They can cook fish, shrimp Creole and crab leg in a piquant sauce."

The old man laughed, "I think you'll want to save a small plate for Mr. Willie for the directions."

"Who is Mister Willy, sir?" I naively asked.

"Well, that would be me. Mr. Eldridge Thaddeus Williams of the Shiloh Church of God and a friend to fishermen and lost souls," he laughed.

Unsure as to whether he was joking, I said, "Well, it is a pleasure to meet a fellow man of the cloth Mr. Willy," and wrote his name down on the small notebook I always carried in my back pocket.

"So you a preacher too," he looked at me with a quizzical look.

"Not yet sir, working on it. But a handshake among those that share and inspire others to receive the grace of God, can be sure the promise will be kept," I underscored repeating a phrase I had heard from a Baptist preacher at a nearby church in Maryland and memorized. With such verbiage and flare, maybe he would also ask me to preach a little at his church, as my dreams of becoming an **Adventist Minister were still high on my priority list.**

"See here--and by the way what's your name--?"

"My name is Santiago Mena," I replied.

"Well, that is what I call an impressive name. Yes, sir. Well, Santa…Sen-ti…What does that name mean in English?"

"It means James, Mr. Willy."

Well, then, Mr. Jim Mena, I am giving you this plastic five-gallon bucket of chicken necks, blessed to be fruitful and bring forth many blue crab from our waters." He chuckled, since to Willie this had become a fun game with a talkative child who tried to equal his enthusiasm for crabbing and followed his every word.

"Agreed, Mr. Willie. We'll bring you some Cuban creole food for helping us catch the crabs."

"I trust you, Jim. I know you'll be back with my meal tomorrow morning. Now shake." We shook hands and I carried the heavy five-gallon bucket now partially filled to about a quarter its capacity with chicken feet and necks.

Mom had finished her shopping and drove up to where I stood outside the store with large plastic bucket held by both hands.

"What's that?" She asked.

After I explained to my mother about my conversation with the black, southern man and packed the chicken necks inside the trunk of the Ford, Mr. Williams stood in front of our car.

"You must be Jim's

momma." "Jim?" she asked.

"Yes. I can't pronounce that *Santinago* name, so I call him Jim—no disrespect."

"Okay,"

My mother looked on wearily waiting for the man to go on, although she would not have understood anyway given her limited ability to communicate in English.

"You see ma'am, he's got everything he needs to go crabbing, but he forgot one thing," he explained. "He doesn't know where to go, so I drew a little map here for the boy and whoever will be driving."

"Thank you," she said.

"All I ask is that you don't share it with anybody else," he said winking at me as if sharing a secret. My mother instructed me to thank the gentleman for his help and assure him that we would follow his map to the letter.

"Oh, yes ma'am, Jim will also tell you about our deal."

"Okay. Thank you," she replied automatically. "*Qué dice ese señor?*" she asked.

My mother engaged the 62 Ford on drive and stepped on the gas making a run for the kitchenette hotel. She was mad.

"What in the name of the Bible have you done? What did you promise that man?" She yelled. To my surprise, she understood the word deal and wanted to know what I had agreed to do for him.

"I told him we would take him a bowl of shrimp or crab with some rice and bread as a gift for sharing his fishing hole."

"Did you tell him where we're staying?"

"Of course not, momma, I would never do that."

"Well, we better find your father and your uncles.

Esto me huele mal."

Of course, everything smelled bad to my mom. Her way of saying I had made a mistake and that now there would be consequences of some sort. At the time, I found her to be paranoid and hyper vigilant—even before I learned the meaning of the words. Later in life, I found I suffer from Post-Traumatic-Stress-Disorder which in retrospect make her concerned reaction to almost everything appear mild and sane. My younger brother, Ralph, and myself both depended on counseling sessions as adults to attempt to deprogram the synoptic rewiring that took place during the years prior to our departure from Cuba.

In 1967, my father had been summoned to talk to Cuba's Minister of Industry, An Argentine named Ernesto Guevara, better known to the world as "El *Ché* Guevara". The components for the U.S. manufactured machinery that arrived at our house had been traced. The key components were verified as having been delivered to my father at our home on Apodaca Street. Pepe Mena would be give one last chance to produce the components. When he failed to do so, he was put on a truck to Matanzas that same day. He would be one more volunteer in the sugar cane fields.

A few days later, I came home and my mother was gone. She too had been taken to the fields a couple of hours away without notice. It left four-year-old Ralph in my care on and off for the next year, except when my mother would escape and make an illicit run to our home to see her children and give us the food she had set aside for us; mostly guava paste and crackers.

While we were in Virginia Beach, our point of reference as to what could harm us was still being decided on experiences learned on an island 90-miles south of Florida, and a world away.

We parked in front of the weekly rental apartment where my dad and my uncles were waiting, as well as my cousins Tony and Albert. I hoped I had not made a mistake that would cause us some sort of trouble. Fear was still a constant at my side, that at times took a little time off.

"*Oyé*," said Tony. "We got plenty of chicken necks to really go after them."

"And my friend gave me a little map showing where we can go," I added.

Tony looked it over and shared it with his father, Julián.

"That's the spot," Julián said after reading the handwritten lines on the envelope as if reading Magellan's naval charts. His passion was discovering new places—especially isolated, out-of-the way places.

"The problem with this country is that they have too many people everywhere you go," he would pronounce longing for the solitude and isolation in which he had lived most of his life.

Glancing again at the map he said, "I drove by there two or three times this morning. There's nobody there and we can have the place to ourselves. We'll just need to buy some fishing nets with long poles to bring the crabs into the baskets—and by the way, we need to find two or three more of those plastic buckets."

Julián never bought anything. His phrase was, "we need to find some of..." whatever was needed. Remarkably, he knew that great things of use were thrown away all around us. He was the first conservationist I ever met, even if he didn't know he was one.

We went back to the store and my friend Mr. Willie gave us buckets and directed us to the best place to buy our crabbing and fishing supplies. While at the store, olive oil was purchased with onions, and of course, green peppers, yellow peppers and red peppers—The Holy Trinity of Creole cuisine whether in Louisiana, Jamaica, Puerto Rico, Dominican Republic or Cuba. We returned to the weekly rental that served as our home-away-from-home in Virginia Beach and washed and cut the needed ingredients in preparation for tonight's feast—thanks to my preacher friend, Mr. Minister Eldridge Thaddeus Williams of the Shiloh Church of God. A friend our family came to know well and with whom we often shared a taste of our crab harvest.

"Amen," I said.

CHAPTER 26

A New Religion
And a Small Miracle

During a subsequent visit to New Jersey shortly before the start of the school year in 1971, Azalea and Amelia talked to my mother about having been converted to the "Mormon Church". My mother, a religious woman by nature wanted to know more, surprised at my cousins' sudden interest in religion. She learned that two young men had stopped by their apartment and taught them about this church of which they had never heard before.

Amelia and Azalea also talked about some of the basic tenets of their new faith, as best as they could explain it. My mother asked, "Is this church in D.C. too?" Azalea said that she believed so, adding that she would ask the missionaries to send someone to our home so that they could answer our questions.

A few days later two missionaries knocked on our door. Since my father was not home, they were told to come back another time, as mom had to ask my father if he would allow them to come in and teach my brother and me about their religion. They said they would do so and left two pamphlets with her. One was *The Testimony of the*

Prophet Joseph Smith.

I asked my mother about the young men and how they could be pastors at such a young age. I had often contemplated being an Adventist minister. Preaching the Gospel with vim and vigor to an excited congregation where "Amen" would be offered by the faithful stirred by my words in sermons riddled with references of overcoming life's vicissitudes and replete of inspiration morsels of scripture leading to spiritual salvation. But, then again, I also wanted to play first base for the Washington Senators and bring home the winning run after one of Frank Howard's thundering long balls.

She explained that Amelia had told her that these young men served voluntarily for two years teaching the Gospel throughout the world. I thought the potential of being a minister at that age was an incredible achievement, one I wanted to experience, even if I did not know anything about their Church.

"You could end up in Peru or Central America," mom said.

"Do you get to choose?" I inquired.

"I don't know…I think so."

I wanted to preach as those men I so admired, the Adventist pastors, but doing so anywhere outside of the U.S. was not an option, lest I be returned to Cuba.

"Well, I think I'll have to learn more about it," I said matter of fact as if pondering some great decision.

My mother asked my father about having the missionaries in our home. He agreed on the condition that his presence was not required and that the missionaries would not talk to him during their visits. The animosity my father held at the time for organized religion was a carry-over following my mother's excommunication from her Adventist congregation in Cuba.

On a cold September evening two young men who spoke Spanish with a heavy American accent knocked on our door. Their names were Elder George Michael Bean of Eugene, Oregon and Elder Marc Henry from Bountiful, Utah. My mother welcomed them into our home and explained that they were free to teach her children and her, but that my father was not to be engaged, even if he chose to sit and join us. They agreed.

For the next three weeks they visited our home twice a week at my mother's request. After the first visit, my father would prepare a meal and ask them to join us for dinner. They did, but never discussed religion and limited themselves to mollifying my father's curiosity.

Dad had learned that they volunteered their time and were not professional ministers, although "duly authorized priesthood holders," as they would emphasize. My father was not interested in such things that appeared to be so important to them as tracing their authority to the Lord himself. He was more concerned with important and practical things such as "where do you boys eat?"

Learning that they were not from Maryland and that they cooked for themselves or ate with families when invited, my father could not bear to see them not have a proper home-cooked meal at least a couple of times a week. Dad also insisted they bring others whenever possible, so that he could feed them too.

"They are so young," he said to my mom.

"They need someone to take care of them. I don't want anything to do with their religion, but I would like to feed them. It's the right thing to do," my father reasoned.

If one believes in small miracles, and I do, then what followed, in my estimation qualifies as such. Prior to one of their visits, my father had to be taken by ambulance to Prince George's Hospital for an emergency hernia operation. After his surgery he returned home and was unable to work for a few days while he recovered from his surgery.

I was particularly concerned about him, as he seemed weak and affected by the medical procedure. Every day or every other day my father would give me fifty cents and send me to the Seven-Eleven one block away on Piney Branch Road, just a few yards from the recreation center where we lived most of the summer, to buy him cigarettes.

The son of a tobacco farmer, my father had been a smoker from age seven. My running this errand was something I relished—not for the cigarettes, but because he would allow me to keep the change and buy a candy bar. My favorite, at first, was Milky Way, but after seeing the commercial with a vendor at a circus who with an elephant behind him proclaimed that there was a handful of peanuts in every bar, I became a Snickers man; that is until the calypso beat of Mounds and Almond Joy made me ponder if sometimes *I felt like a nut and sometimes I did not.*

That was the same reason I drank the 7-Up the un-cola. Its deep-voiced pitchman was a fellow islander. I could tell from his rich delivery accentuated with Caribbean happy time speak that he was one of ours. He spoke to me and made me feel cool. "He is one of us," I thought, and so he was—one of ours. He obviously knew what I liked.

A few days after the surgery dad had not sent me to buy him cigarettes. I volunteered to do so. His reply is the best example of hypnotic suggestion I've ever encountered.

"No. I don't smoke anymore."

"Why?" I asked.

"Well, they gave me this gas to make me stop smoking.

So I don't smoke anymore."

I was shocked. How could it be possible? But then, maybe this was one of those miraculous inventions we had heard about, most of which I now found to be of dubious origin or exaggerations. Apparently, this one I had never heard about, the "no-smoking gas" must be true.

Nonetheless, I was saddened by the loss of my candy bars. How would I manage my addiction to chocolate without the cigarette runs? Dad looked at me and smiled.

"There is some change in my pant pocket. Why don't you go get a chocolate bar for yourself and get one for your brother?" I hugged him. Not because of the chocolate, but because I then realized my father loved me and knew the desires of my heart. He was my dad, not just my father.

A couple of days later, Elders Bean and Henry returned. They pulled out their binder from which they taught us. This night they would introduce us to the principle of tithing. I looked at my parents. No reaction. Surely, I deduced, my father was going to throw them out. This was a touchy subject for reasons already explained. However, there was no reaction. My father continued to listen, as he had now done since the third visit. My mother also showed no reaction. Then, Elder Bean proceeded to explain what he called, *The Word of Wisdom*. Well, that was it. Something my father would find objectionable, until I realized he no longer smoked. But, what about his sip or two of rum with Uncle Fermín or the occasional beer while watching the Senators or the Orioles? Apparently, that would not be an issue either.

Last, came the question— the challenge.

"Mrs. Mena, Jorge, Ralph, we would like to extend you a challenge to be baptized in the Church of Jesus Christ of Latter-day Saints: the restored and true Church of God on Earth."

My mind had been made long ago and I knew what my answer would be. I remember being overcome with an indescribable overwhelming feeling while reading the Joseph Smith story that had shaken me to the core with an unequivocal feeling that the Church was true. I had been converted from that moment. I hoped I would be asked to join the Church. I felt as if I belonged, even though we had not yet been to a single service.

We were asked to attend church the following Sunday. This request had made by the missionaries from the third visit. However, my father had made other plans to spend Sundays with Uncle Fermín and Julian and Cora in their Arlington, Virginia home. These were weekly family gatherings, complete with a wonderful dinner prepared by my dad and my uncles, so a visit to Church had not yet happened.

We looked at one another afraid to answer, to commit to anything without dad's approval. The missionaries waited for our response. I think they would have waited all night until their question was answered.

"I don't know about you guys," chimed my dad without fanfare, "but I'm getting baptized."

Elder Henry looked on, mouth agape. Elder Bean had the proverbial deer in the headlights look. My mother cried with joy and hugged him. She sobbed uncontrollably. Ralph and I joined her in the warm and wonderful family embrace. We had been told that families could live together for time and all eternity, that families are forever. This was the moment when our family took its first step in hopes of being worthy to realize such a promise. We wanted to be a family, forever.

Now, the moment that explained dad's smoking cessation with one easy dose of magical "no-smoking gas":

Uncle Fermín had been taken to the Washington Adventist Hospital because of trouble with his ulcers. He was hospitalized for two nights. Mom and dad immediately were at his side the next day after coming home from work and picking Ralph and me up from school.

While we visited him in his hospital room, my father pointed to the metal plate on the wall to which a small, green plastic hose was attached with a breathing mask at the end. Black plastic letters glued to the metal square spelled: "No Smoking."

"Fermín, do you want to stop smoking?" Dad asked.

"No, why?" Fermín replied.

"Because they have the treatment here too if you want to stop smoking. It's right there over the bed."

Doctor Miguel Rodriguez who had become a close

friend of our family, as well as our physician, walked in, thus the conversation had abruptly come to an end as he checked Fermin's vitals and talked to the family. The conversation about "no-smoking gas" had not continued, for which I later was very grateful. My curiosity was piqued.

"Doctor Rodriguez," I asked as I followed him as he left the room. "How does the treatment to stop smoking work?"

Puzzled, he asked, "What treatment?"

"The 'No Smoking' treatment over the bed," I replied.

"Oh, that, that is just oxygen for patients who need help breathing. Much like your dad after his surgery when he was coming out of the anesthetic," he explained plainly, as if I should have known.

Dr. Rodriguez always spoke in medical terms and assumed we understood his explanations. Honestly, that only happened about half the time.

A small miracle had taken place indeed. Needless to say, this elucidation was never shared with my father.

CHAPTER 27

A Most Peculiar Sunday

Our first visit to the Church of Jesus Christ of Latter-day Saints was different from what I had expected. Having been raised in the Adventist faith, although never having been baptized, I had set expectations of what Church services should be.

As we arrived at the Washington, D.C. Latin American Branch on 16th Street and Columbia Road in the Adams Morgan neighborhood of our nation's capital. It was just a few blocks from the White House, where 16th Street and Pennsylvania Avenue intersect. Our first response was, "this is a very dangerous place," and quietly asked ourselves if our car would be there after services.

We entered the beautiful old building with a bronze statue of the Angel Moroni on its steeple, only one of a handful of these statues in the world at the time, and the only one not on an LDS temple in 1971. We were mesmerized by the uniqueness of the building.

Elders Bean and Henry introduced us to people who would become lifelong friends: Carlos Gamarra from Bolivia, Juan Fajardo, Sr., from Guatemala and Evaristo Rojas from Colombia. We also met Alberto Molina and his family, including his daughter Sandra whom I was surprised to see there as we had attended school together since the fifth grade.

They were friendly and welcomed us into the fold. English-language services were being held in the building at the same time as ours.

"The LDS Church must be the largest Church in Washington, D.C.," I said to my dad, as I had never seen services held concurrently in one building in two languages; either that or they did not have much money and were sharing space because they could not afford two buildings. Whatever the answer, it was fine with me, things of the Spirit don't have to be tied to material things. Besides, I thought, a successful Church will have a large congregation, which is also good.

Robert D. Smith was the Branch President. I immediately concluded that he must have been related to Joseph Smith and to the President of the Church, Joseph Fielding Smith, Junior, whom I had been told was a prophet and also related to the prophet Joseph who was his granduncle.

President. The title was curious, but I concluded it meant he was the pastor.

The Church had some interesting practices, I thought, as I attempted to tie loose ends without asking too many questions as to not be considered impertinent or irreverent at asking such trivial things as, why were there so many men named Elder and Smith?

Was it a requirement to change your name, as my Muslim friend Muhammad had done at joining the Faith of Islam? I hoped I could keep mine. I liked it.

Later that Sunday I met Juan Fajardo, Jr. and his friend Mario Valdivieso. I was somewhat relieved when I learned that they too were converts to the Church—and Hispanics—and that they had not changed their names.

"Today," volunteered Juan Fajardo, Sr., "is a wonderful day. It is fast and testimony meeting."

His smile gave us reassurance that some great spiritual feast was about to take place. I already pictured a fire and brimstone sermon, of the kind I hoped to someday preach, provided I was not playing for the Senators or the Orioles in the bigs, in which case I would have to wait until after my baseball career.

Instead, one by one, members of the congregation—without having been called by our minister—randomly walked up to the pulpit after the opening exercises to speak to the congregation.

Some cried as they talked of their love of the Gospel and how it guided their lives.

Others shared moments of trial overcome by faith and prayer. Some offered their gratitude to Heavenly Father and His Son Jesus Christ and for their guidance, love and influence in making the important decisions in their lives. It was an unexpected and most unique spectacle, I thought. These were a most peculiar people. But, then, so were we.

Our decision to be baptized was reaffirmed, until I realized that maybe, after we joined the Church, we too had to go to the microphone and speak. It was at that moment that I decided that baseball was a more apt calling and vocation than being a pastor, as it did not require public speaking.

Fortunately, the meeting was called to a close and my prayers of not having to speak in public were answered. When we left Church that day, we had discovered that our new Church was unique: it was loving and kind and it was where we belonged.

On October second of 1971, Elder George Michael Bean baptized my father, mother and younger brother. I asked the quiet and stoic Elder Mark Henry to baptize me.

In the coming years, the Church would transform all our lives. My father would finally learn to read at a proficient level after having been called to serve in a volunteer leadership position as Branch Clerk. When reluctant to accept his calling at first because of his limited education, he was assured that the Lord would prepare him to fulfill his calling. He was told that the Lord was calling him to serve, not President Smith, even as Aaron of the Old Testament was called to serve. A man of faith, he accepted and developed skills he never thought he would master. Dad became a voracious reader of scripture, until suffering a stroke that limited his abilities late in life. He also became a powerful speaker who communicated with simple words and a strong spirit.

Nearly half a century later after our conversion and baptism, their impact and their testimony continues be felt in our family. Following my father's example, I married in the temple with the promise of an eternal family, if worthy of such a blessing. Two of my six sons have served missions in Mexico, much as those two young Elders who knocked on our door.

Mom and dad died strong in the faith that we would be reunited again as an eternal family and live together for time and all eternity. Just as I too have faith that my own wife and children will be reunited with me and share in that same eternal promise.

CHAPTER 28

The Virginia Beach
Crabbing Extravaganza of '72

We followed Julian's blue 1971 Chevy Impala. He wore his usual knee-high shorts that once served as his construction work pants. On the radio the Fortunes played "Here Comes That Rainy Feeling Again," my favorite song of the summer, although Paul McCartney's "Hands Across the Water" and Olivia Newton John's "If Not for You," seemed to outplay it almost three-to-one. My portable AM/ FM radio with telescopic antenna and faux leather cover was never more than an arm's length away. Music had been—and continues to be—a great part of my life; although my playlist stopped around 1983, save for a few more recent hits that somehow have made it into the mp3 player on my smartphone.

But that summer of 1972 was when our family fell in love again with Virginia Beach. Mornings were spent on the beach swimming, listening to music and girl watching.

Afternoons found us on our crabbing paradise casting multiple lines of about 10 to 12 yards of fishing line with a chicken neck attached at the end.

These were spaced a few feet from one another and tied to a stick we drove in the soft clay shore.

While waiting to retrieve the lines, most with a crab feasting on its chicken bait, we ate Lay's potato chips, drank small cans of Coke and fished; not that I can remember anyone ever catching any fish during our crab hunts.

Willy, Cora and Julian's youngest son was in diapers at the time and was seemingly always in my arms or tugging at my leg. My other cousins and I became skilled hunters of the Chesapeake hard-shelled delights that would end up in a Creole piquant sauce within hours of enjoying their last meal of chicken necks.

Dozens were transported in plastic five-gallon buckets filled to the brim. I'm sure that if we had contacted the Guinness World Records folks and had them watch us devour the vast pots of crab served with steamed rice and French bread, we would have been awarded some record.

After dinner, our family would walk to the boardwalk and stroll for a leisurely moonlight excursion. My cousins and me, without exception, found ourselves on the beach outside of the Peppermint Beach Club listening to the live music that emanated from inside. Some evenings, bands of lesser renown would play outside the club.

And, thus, our family gathered at Virginia Beach for summers to come, until Fermín, Julián and their families left for Miami, Florida seeking to find their riches. The adage of families and business not being a good mix proved true. Instead or riches, they found a severing of family ties because of a financial dispute that lasted for nearly three decades, until 2009 when I took my wife and five of my six sons on a Florida vacation.

It was during that visit that I was told, when asking about Julián, that he had committed suicide rather than continue suffering from the cancer that overwhelmed him. It was a shocking revelation.

"We thought we would tell in you in person," my cousin Liliana said. "I'm so sorry," she offered.

Julian was an impulsive man with an exaggerated sense of privacy and exceedingly bad temper. He ruled over his family with an iron fist. My aunt, Cora and my cousin, Marisol, were kept practically prisoners in their own home, as he tried to protect them from harm and "evil influences."

I did not see him for nearly a decade, as he had distanced himself from everyone, becoming more paranoid with age. Nonetheless, I loved him, as did his family and my memories of the great crabbing extravaganza of 1972 are the images with which I chose to remember him.

CHAPTER 29

My Father and the Atomic Rat

The 1960s and 1970s were a time of change. Some say a time when our country matured. A time of social evolution when demonstrations were all the rage: anti-nuclear demonstrations, peace demonstrations, anti-Nixon demonstration, demonstrations against the Viet-Nam war—and of course, a time of hippies and of the Watergate break-in.

Television channels were limited, even in our nation's capital, to the three network stations and PBS's WETA on the hard-to-find UHF channel 26. Nonetheless, there was never a shortage of vivid images on the evening news. My father, not an avid follower of the news, did occasionally watch these broadcasts mostly for the purpose of exercising his own First Amendment rights.

"Those long-haired hippies are a bunch of communists," he would opine in erudite fashion, "what they need to do is get a job and thank God for living in this country," he would continue. "If they were in Cuba, they'd be slaving in the cane fields."

Having experienced those fields of which he spoke, he found them to be the ultimate punishment.

Incensed by these "ungrateful people," as he called them, he failed to realize that it was that right to stand freely, shake one's fist at the seed of power in Washington and chant anti- government slogans that were part and parcel of the freedoms we so desperately longed to have in the land of our birth. We did not comment on his pontifications. He was dad and he spoke from his heart not knowing his words were a reflection of the same First Amendment that allowed those comments and demonstrations he found so upsetting.

Our family had now lived in the United States for over five years and we had moved to our new house at 8011 18th Avenue, Langley Park, Maryland. It was a beautiful, small, three-bedroom brick house with a spacious backyard.

The move had had other benefits, more than just being in a house, instead of an apartment—although we had purchased a townhouse two years earlier prior to my father deciding he wanted us to live in Provo, Utah, a place he had not ever seen, much less visited.

That move—that lasted only the length of the trip from our recently sold home in Maryland to Provo, where we stayed for two whole days, before returning back to Maryland, resulted in our moving into an apartment for over a year in Forestville, Maryland, until the purchase of our new home.

Being an enterprising man, my father decided to build a family room in our new house. An addition he could build himself.

To accomplish this on a budge, he would do most of the work with friends from church, my brother and me.

One late evening, in the middle of the construction of the new addition he sat at our kitchen table admiring his work. Hearing the crashing of his chair to the floor along with a glass of juice, we rushed to the kitchen. Dad was pale.

"What's the matter, Pepe?" my mother asked.

"It's a monster," he explained.

"A monster?" Ralph asked.

"Yes. I've never seen such a hideous creature in my life," he continued.

"It is a rat, but it is deformed. I think it has been exposed to nuclear power," he went on.

"It has a long snout and razor-sharp teeth that protrude from its mouth. It's tail in long and bare. And it is more than a foot long."

We were frightened. My father had never feared man nor beast.

"What are we going to do, Dad?" I

asked. "We have to kill it," he said.

"How?" Ralph wanted to

know. "I don't know," he

answered.

That night dad took the evening watch seated at the kitchen table once again with a baseball bat at hand to ensure our safety. The next day, when he arrived from work, we drove to a toy store in Langley Park. He bought a toy bow and arrow set that he converted from toy to weapon by removing the rubber suction cups at the end of each arrow and sharpening each wooden projectile until creating a tip sure to penetrate the horrendous monster.

That night the monster returned. Father was ready for it and he fired each arrow at the creature, but failed to hit his mark. Our unfinished family room had become a thoroughfare for the beast.

Night after night, it would return and my father would fire his arrows and later BBs from his newly acquired BB gun. As the atomic rat— as my father had christened the pest—had not threatened us and did not seem interested in entering our home, it became a source of nightly entertainment as dad fired whatever weapon he had improvised while subjecting it to a myriad of curse words and damnations in our native tongue.

Finally, one night, while we watched a University of Maryland vs. Wake Forest basketball game on TV, dad decided to get some snacks during halftime. For reason unbeknownst to us, except for maybe anticipating another encounter with the creature, he had armed himself with a new weapon at the ready in his pocket: a baseball. That bullet made by Spalding accomplished what no other ordnance had been able to do. It struck the beast knocking it senseless in our unfinished addition. In keeping with the baseball theme of the evening, my father grabbed the bat he kept by the door and finished the job.

"You're right," my mother said as she analyzed the fallen creature. "It is deformed."

Ralph suggested we call the police and I agreed. Eduardo Lugo, a young member of our congregation arrived shortly thereafter to visit our family. He had been close by at the Spanish-language radio station and made a detour on the way home.

Excitedly, we answered the door and invited him to see the atomic rat that he had heard so much about from dad.

"That's not a rat," he declared.

"I know, it doesn't look like one; it's deformed," dad exclaimed.

"No, Brother Mena, you're mistaken. It is an opossum."

I had heard the word from Granny while watching the Beverly Hillbillies, but had no idea what it was or what it looked like.

"I think some people eat it," I said in shock. "Who?" Dad inquired.

"Hillbillies," I replied.

"Like Granny and Jethro," Ralph said.

"Like Granny and Jethro," my mother laughed.

And so ended the great hunt for the atomic rat that terrorized my father for the better part of a month in the fall of 1974 in our new house by the creek in Langley Park, Maryland.

CHAPTER 30

WFAN-FM
La Grande

It was through Eduardo Lugo that I visited WFAN-FM. The station was Washington, D.C.'s first and only Spanish-speaking station for many years. Eduardo loved the magic of radio. Those whose voices were broadcast on the 100.3 frequency on the FM dial were the stars and purveyors of a nostalgic connection to the homeland for the tens of thousands of Spanish-speaking listeners in the D.C. metropolitan area. The station's coverage also included neighboring cities in Maryland and Virginia. For my friend, it was more of "theater in the mind," than a source of music and information. He actually saw himself behind the old RCA ribbon microphone delivering a mesmerizing narrative that would hold every listener spellbound, and just when his words would move them, he would punctuate the moment with the most apt song for said moment. There was only one problem: Eduardo Lugo had a heavy Puerto Rican accent and a high-pitched, nasal voice atypical of any announcer on the radio. The Lord had chosen not to bless him with an announcers' voice, the greatest desire of his heart.

On the other hand, I had been speaking in a deep baritone since around age 12; the first time I recall impersonating my father on the phone as the caller assumed the bass-rich on the other end of the line belonged to a rugged adult, rather than the 115 lbs. boy with the unusually incongruous voice for someone his age. It was Eduardo's notice of my unusually deep voice that lead him to invite me to visit his friends at the radio station; as a sort of show-and-tell oddity.

The station was located on First Ave., N.E. in an old brick building with two gargantuan radio towers—one holding the transmitter antenna to WFAN-FM, and the second one to WOOK-AM. To me, this was a remarkable site, and, unbeknownst to me at the time, the start of my broadcast and journalism career.

It was a Saturday afternoon. Eduardo who had been visiting our home, as he often did, invited me to accompany him to the station. He spent hours practicing his announcing skills in the production studio that separated the soul station from its Spanish-language sister broadcast.

As we entered the building we took a small dark staircase just to the right of the main door whose keys dangled from the inside on the opposite side of the keyhole. He had telephoned ahead "not on the listeners' line," he proudly pronounced, but on the private line that blinked directly over the console. Israel Interiano del Castillo the gently and affable Honduran who would become one of my closest friends for the coming years, opened the door and greeted us both as if we were old friends.

"I have to run. The record is almost over," he pronounced in the most melodious and impressive voice I had ever heard.

We followed hastily, lest the record end due to our delaying the master of the airwaves that afternoon.

Just at the top of the stairs was a hallway, but rather than follow it to the door just a few feet down and on the right, we entered through the small studio that held the largest record collection I had ever seen. Interiano, as he preferred to be called, threw a small switch to the right on the old board and adjusted the red dial that controlled the volume of his voice. The VU meter pegged as if overpowered by the man's voice; actually it slightly distorted the voice by over modulating it, a term I would hear often mentioned over the coming years by Steve, the short, thin, square-dance aficionado that served as the stations' chief engineer. He too would become an influence and a teacher in my life that would impart lessons never to be forgotten; some even having to do with radio broadcasting.

It was an afternoon filled with wonder, almost magical. This would be my world. I had never been so sure of anything in my life as I was at that moment in a gray autumn afternoon in 1974. Without being asked, I brought water, coffee, records, cleaned and replaced the used discs on their respective sleeves and without uttering the slightest sound, listened to every word spoken by every one of the men who came in and out of *Radio La Grande* well into the evening.

At some point that afternoon, someone asked me to go to the bathroom and rip the wire for the upcoming newscast. At seeing my perplexed expression,

Eduardo explained in his best didactic demeanor that the wire was the copy coming over the teletype housed, oddly enough, in the facilities. I went around the corner, entered the small room and after rolling a large amount of the yellow teletype paper in my arm, waited for the incoming story to end and ripped it off the spool. It was news, and so I assumed that time was of the essence, so I ran to the small studio door ensuring to enter stealthily as to not interrupt the art emanating from the adjoining broadcast booth.

Interiano jokingly said, "find me some good stories,"
.... ending his words in midsentence at the realization he did not know my name.

"Santiago Jorge Mena," I quickly replied. Israel Interiano del Castillo was a formal and regal name. I should have one too, I thought.

"Okay, Santiaguito, find me a good lead and a few more for the news at the top of the hour. Okay?" I nodded. Then, a most peculiar event took place.

"You have them?" the announcer asked. "Yes," I nodded.

"Read them to me," he followed.

I found his unusual request somewhat puzzling. Was he testing my ability to read Spanish? Was he auditioning me? I found both hard to digest, but did as asked and read the copy.

"Muy bién, *muchachito*," he said with a proud smile somewhat taken aback by my ability to read Spanish and the unanticipated tenor of my voice.

The song ended. He pressed a green button of what appeared to be an eight-track tape that fired the station's news jingle. He dialed the volume down and almost simultaneously opened the microphone and the magic of radio took a different turn. Israel Interiano del Castillo barely read the paper in front of him. He repeated the words I had read to him as if playing back a recording. My new friend with the magical voice had an impressive recall and a powerful delivery; good, because he could not read at a level beyond that of a second grader. This truly was theater of the mind. My introduction to my chosen profession had begun.

CHAPTER 31

Merry Radio Christmas!

I quickly became a regular fixture at the station from morning to night, or so it seemed. My father, a supportive man by nature, relished in my success.

"My son works at the radio station," he would proudly share with anyone within earshot of whatever was being broadcast on any radio.

In reality, it was more of an unpaid internship, but within a few weeks, I could be found sitting in control of the board playing records and commercials during station meetings or while waiting to switch from our live broadcasts to "*La Novela Goya*" with its captivating figures, suspenseful narrative and overly dramatic acting.

I had become friends with every one of the announcers, including the station manager, Estuardo Valdermar, the Peruvian-born owner of a print shop in the Adams Morgan neighborhood of Washington, D.C. Proficient at transferring records to tape-caster tape cartridges that served as a primitive form of broadcast automation in the seventies, I became useful. It was there that I also learned to find pertinent news copy from the teletype and to even complete sentences typing below rows of blue where the teletype had been stuck due to the paper not being correctly fed, thus resulting in incomplete news stories. It was Valdemar, as we called him, who on Christmas Eve of 1974 gave me one of the greatest gifts of my life.

"Aren't you going to call your parents?" he asked.

"Why?" I asked confused.

"I thought they might want to hear you on the radio at 6," he smiled.

"Mom, Dad! Listen to the news. I'm going on the air with Valdemar!"

I hung up before I could hear their response and quickly began to read the barely legible print on the torn yellow pages of the teletype stories.

Six o'clock clicked on the old, loud clock over the glass divider between our control room and the production studio. The news jingle played and Estuardo Valdemar opened the microphone,

"*Muy buenas tardes. Aquí los titulares,*" and he read the headlines. The teaser to the upcoming stories.

"*Les hablan,*" he said pointing at me, "*Santiago Jorge Mena,*" I said voice quivering and hands shaking uncontrollably,

"*… Y Estuardo Valdemar.*"

It was nerve-wrecking, it was unadulterated happiness and it was the worst newscast of my career. But, I was happy. I was overjoyed to the point of feeling euphoric.

"Thank you!" I yelled jumping and running in place in the tiny booth.

"You're welcome." He said. "Merry Christmas."

It was the merriest of Christmas. And while circumstances and diverging interests over the coming years lead to a distancing, perhaps even an end to our friendship. I will forever be grateful to a kind man who made a Christmas Eve many years ago an unforgettable moment for a teen boy with a dream of broadcast greatness and a thankful heart.

CHAPTER 32

The Meeting

My junior year of high school was my last year of high school due to my early graduation. My broadcast career was in its embryonic stages. I was allowed to leave school during fifth period so that I could be at the station by 2:30. Credit would be granted for my work at WFAN toward my elective credits for graduation. I would take the bus just across High Point High School on Riggs Road and ride it to First Street every Monday through Friday.

On this particular day, Iván Quiñonez, the station manager greeted me in the small parking lot in front of the station while smoking a cigarette.

"Santiaguito," he said, "I need you to sit in the control room while I talk to Jorge for a few minutes."

"No problem," I nodded, "Always happy to sit behind the board," I said.

"Oh," he added, "lock the door once he leaves the booth and don't let him back in under any circumstance, you understand?"

I nodded with a puzzled look. We both walked upstairs, me to the production studio where records and tape cartridges awaited me and Iván to his office. The phone in the production control room lit up.

"Yes." I answered.

"Santiaguito, tell Jorge I need to see him and do as I told you," said Mr. Quiñonez on the phone. I did as told.

I placed the log just above the board by the binder with the PSAs and live spots and carefully played the commercials indicated in the document in between records. It wasn't long before the shouting could be heard, followed by a loud door slamming against the door frame and a loud banging on the broadcast booth.

"Open this damned door, Santiago," Jorge shouted.

"I need to say goodbye to my audience," said Jorge almost in poetic tone.

He had been fired over a word. That's right: a word, not over words.

Jorge Paucar Salazar was a small, religious man from Ecuador with a gentle demeanor and an uncharacteristic passive-aggressive relationship with our station manager, Iván Quiñonez. It all started over an escalating dispute over the word "company" or *compañía* in Spanish, which many in Ecuador pronounce as companía, softening the "ñ" in the word. This mispronounced word became the source of contention between the two men. Finally, Iván had had enough; especially after Jorge went out of his way to add the word whenever possible to news copy, or ad libs prior and after songs. I often wondered why the diminutive man was so enamored of such a boring word with many better sounding synonyms. On this day, the word ended his broadcast career, at least in our nation's capital.

For me, however, it provided an unexpected opportunity that lead to a lifetime of professional bliss.

In the heat of the moment, Iván hastily left the building shortly after Jorge Paucar Salazar and I was left the sole person at the station, thus, the one in charge, as I saw it.

After a brief call home asking my brother to crank the volume on the radio once tuned to WFAN-FM, I opened the microphone's volume controlling "pot" and with the calm and demeanor of an experienced broadcaster, began to read news, live commercials and PSAs—recorded ones be damned—and proceeded to segue and lead-in in between songs, dutifully giving the time and weather forecast at the indicated times on the face of the clock facing me from just above the glass divider between the studios. It was Christmas all over again, but this time I was ready.

Eventually, the business line blinked and I answered it anticipating a fate comparable to that of Jorge's earlier that afternoon.

"I thought I said not to go on the air," said Iván in a calm tone.

"Yes you did, Mr. Quiñonez, but people were wondering why no one was talking on the air, and I thought you would want me to do so...for the sake of the listeners," I retorted attempting to convince myself, although the comments about the callers were true.

There was a long silence on the line and finally our boss spoke.

"Okay. We could do worse, although not by much," he commented.

"You got the spot starting tomorrow, but don't be late!"

The line went dead as my career in broadcasting came to life; even if at minimum wage.

A few months later, I suggested we add a morning news show with me hosting, of course. Ivan agreed.

"Great idea," he said, "it will give us a chance to get somebody in here to teach you some real Spanish."

A few days later, María Elena Guerra, my mentor, my friend, became the anchor of the newly created morning news program.

A few months later, I graduated high school. Many of my childhood friends, had moved away by then; mostly to Florida. It was at about this time that I realized that my American Transformation had almost completely taken place and that the time of wonderment had nearly come to a close as well.

CHAPTER 33

Epilog

I left for Los Angeles a few weeks after graduating high school. There I realized that my American transformation was such that it would never come to a total completion as, at least in my case, it is an ongoing process.

The transformation continued as I attended Glendale College, joined the United Sates Air Force Reserves, married, saw my first child be born, and worked in television, international marketing—traveling throughout Latin America—moving back to Washington, D.C. working for the Voice of America, the same international broadcast organization my father and I listened to clandestinely in my childhood and eventually worked at TV and Radio Martí as its program and news director allowing my fellow Cubans to have access to a free press.

More than 50 years later, from the time I first stepped on the hallowed ground of my beloved adoptive country, I've raised six sons, have two grandsons and a granddaughter whom I love beyond measure, and have lived a remarkably blessed life.

And at every benchmark in my life, I've heard my parents' voices: "Anything is possible in this country. This is your new home. Love her and make it better by you becoming better. The word impossible has no meaning in our beloved America."

As Bonasera said, *I love America. America has made my fortune. And I have raised six sons in the American fashion.*

My cousin, Liliana, with "Abue" and me 1960. Marta and me with our twin cousins in the background. My parents and me in our first picture taken in the U.S. 13 Feb., 1969. My uncles José and Fermín (L-R) New Jersey 1971. Basement dance 1972. Cuban pig roast with Fermin, Liliana, Mom, Dad and Julio, summer of 1970.

WFAN-FM, Washington, D.C. with Mario Martinez y Palacios 1974.
WFAN-FM On-Air Studio 1975. My parents visit Provo, Utah 1982.
With fellow airmen at Chanute AFB 1978. Family picture at Fermin's
house in Takoma Park, Maryland Christmas 1971.

On assignment for the Voice of America in Port-au-Prince, Haiti in 1990. Being interviewed while on assignment in Santo Domingo, Dominican Republic, also in 1990.

Michael, Eric, Patrick, Nathan, Alex and Nick 2016

ABOUT THE AUTHOR

S. Mena and his family migrated to the United States from Cuba. He grew up in the Washington, D.C. suburbs of Takoma Park and Silver Spring, Maryland. An award-winning broadcast journalist, Mena covered Latin America and the Caribbean for the United States Information Agency's Voice of America and helped launch two U.S. Government broadcast services specific to Cuba: Radio Martí and TV Martí. He presently resides in Idaho Falls with his wife, Kristin where they raised their six sons.

Made in the
USA
Lexington, KY